NO MAN'S LAND

By CARL COKE RISTER

PUBLISHED BY THE UNIVERSITY OF OKLAHOMA PRESS
NORMAN, OKLAHOMA

Southern Plainsmen, 1938
Border Captives, 1940
Land Hunger, 1942
Border Command, 1944
Robert E. Lee in Texas, 1946
No Man's Land, 1948

&

The Southwestern Frontier, 1865–1881
CLEVELAND, 1928

The Greater Southwest
(*with* R. N. Richardson)
GLENDALE, 1934

Western America
(*with* LeRoy R. Hafen)
NEW YORK, 1941

NO MAN'S LAND

By

CARL COKE RISTER

NORMAN
UNIVERSITY OF OKLAHOMA PRESS
1948

COMPOSED AND PRINTED
BY THE UNIVERSITY OF OKLAHOMA PRESS
AT NORMAN, OKLAHOMA, U.S.A.

To Rupert H. Johnson
Friend

PREFACE

During the late eighteen eighties land-hungry pioneers claimed a High Plains wind-swept zone between Kansas and Colorado on the north and the Texas Panhandle on the south, and the Cherokee country on the east and New Mexico on the west, a region larger than two of the New England states and unoccupied except by cattlemen. This land-orphan was part of that vast area which Texas sold to the federal government by the Compromise of 1850 and which Congress later overlooked when it fixed the boundaries of contiguous states and territories.

But homesteaders had not forgotten it. Since earliest times their wagons on the Santa Fé Trail had crossed its western uplands, or, in more recent times, had moved over the Jones and Plummer Trail to Texas or Kansas. Now they came to "No Man's Land" to build a hardy culture, to change what later they found to be a "Dust Bowl" into a "Wheat Bowl," as a recent press report has so aptly described the transmutation. That these No Man's Land pioneers brought law and order to a land without law, dug a meager subsistence from a wind-blown soil, and survived the extreme hardships of pioneering is surprising enough; but that a residue of them, and their sons and daughters, stayed through the prolonged drought, the "Dirty Thirties," then leveled the sand dunes, revived wheat-growing, and matured a distinctive High Plains way of life is convincing proof of their sturdiness and resourcefulness.

A generous grant-in-aid from the American Philosophical Society made it possible for me to search for No Man's Land materials in several depositories: the Library of Congress; the National Archives; the state libraries of Colorado, Kansas, Oklahoma, and Texas; the University of Oklahoma and the University of Texas libraries; the Lawson Title Company's collection at Beaver and the Panhandle Historical Museum at Goodwell, Oklahoma; and the Phillips Collection of the University of Oklahoma.

In addition, there are surviving No Man's Land pioneers and others who wish to preserve our Western literary heritage who furnished materials or who helped in other ways. Among these are Mr. and Mrs. Fred C. Tracy, Miss Eleanor Tracy, Miss Maud Thomas, and Mr. and Mrs. W. T. Quinn of Beaver, Oklahoma; the late Boss Neff of Hooker, Oklahoma; Mr. and Mrs. Harry Parker of Follett, Texas; John L. McCarty, formerly assistant publisher of the Amarillo *Globe-News;* H. H. Finnell of the Federal Department of Agriculture Conservation Service; and many others.

To the staffs of these several libraries and collections and to those who individually supplied materials or supported my work in other ways, I extend my thanks. And I am deeply grateful to my wife, Mattie May Rister, who two summers past traveled with me from town to town in the Wheat Belt while the temperature registered above one hundred degrees, and helped to transcribe early-day accounts and to catalog my notes. I alone am responsible for any error that inadvertently may appear in this narrative.

Carl Coke Rister

Norman, Oklahoma
April 23, 1948

CONTENTS

ILLUSTRATIONS

NO MAN'S LAND

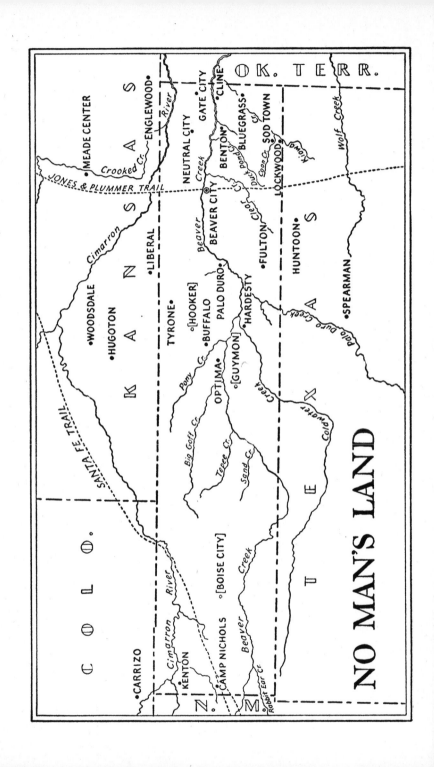

"God's Land, but No Man's"

"**N**o Man's Land! No Man's Land! Read all about it!" This could have been the call of a modern newsboy had he been living in New York City on January 20, 1889, and selling the latest issue of the *Sun*. The *Sun* carried a sensational story of more than one and one-half pages—larger space than had ever been given in previous years to a Western problem. The article told of a land in the West more extensive than the two states of Delaware and Rhode Island, a land which Congress had forgotten, a No Man's Land that was a refuge for outlaws and border riffraff. In addition, the *Sun's* editor wrote a racy editorial under an apt caption, "God's Land, But No Man's."

This story of No Man's Land had been months in the making. On a midwinter day the *New York Sun's* traveling reporter, J. R. Spears, stepped off the stage at Beaver, in No Man's Land, to investigate conditions in this struggling border town. Spears did his work methodically and without fanfare. He talked to townsmen, traveled over the near-by prairies, and interviewed ranchers and squatters. Then he quietly returned to New York. The news of what he had learned appeared in the *Sun*. It was a scoop!

But where was this No Man's Land? In what way had

Congress neglected it? The answers to these questions, and the whole story of a forgotten land were of great interest to American people in 1889, even though the region were in the distant West.

"No Man's Land," also the title of the young reporter's article, was a term popularly applied to a rectangular strip of land in the very heart of the United States. It embraced the present-day Oklahoma Panhandle, and consisted of 5,670 square miles or 3,681,000 acres of land lying on the northern border of the Texas Panhandle.

Why Congress and the American people had forgotten this land is a question easier to ask than to answer. From those lands which Texas brought into the Union in 1845, the territory north of 36 degrees, 30 minutes, was generally regarded as nonslave territory. Five years later, the Compromise of 1850 provided for the present Texas boundaries, and that region between 36 degrees, 30 minutes, and 37 degrees was given up by Texas, since this half a degree was within the free zone, and its loss was of little consequence to the huge new state.

But the problem of slavery would not down, and presently Congress was so preoccupied with it, and in fixing the boundaries of western territories, that it neglected to include No Man's Land in any administrative unit. Consequently, this great area was left unclaimed by any state. It was simply lost in the Great West and sandwiched between Indian Territory on the east, New Mexico on the west, Kansas and Colorado on the north, and the Texas Panhandle on the south.

It seems a paradox that this region should have been slighted, for it was explored early in the history of America. In fact, sixty-six years before the first English colonists landed at Jamestown and seventy-nine years before the Pilgrim Fathers disembarked at Plymouth Rock, a band of thirty Spanish horsemen and six footmen led by the doughty Coronado had crossed these remote wind-swept plains.

While the Spaniards were in New Mexico, a Plains Indian, "El Turco," had sought Coronado to tell him that far to the northeast was the fabulously rich Indian kingdom of Gran Quivira. Coronado believed the story and started toward the new land, using El Turco as his guide. After more than forty days of travel and near-starvation, he came to Gran Quivira, a region of grass houses and well-cultivated fields. He was disappointed at not finding riches, but he did find food—beans, corn, and melons—which was welcome after many days of a buffalo-meat diet. Nevertheless, El Turco had deceived Coronado, and disappointed and angry, the conquistador ordered him garroted for his perfidy.

The explorers then returned to New Mexico, no richer but with a basis for Spain's claim to the Great Plains. The exact route they traveled is not known, but it is fairly certain that it crossed No Man's Land, both in going to and coming from Gran Quivira.

Antonio de Mendoza, the viceroy in Mexico City, had no interest in Gran Quivira and looked on Coronado's expedition as a failure. The conquistador was expected to bring gold, silver, and turquoise to New Spain, and this he had not done. It is not surprising, therefore, that Mendoza and his successors sent no other Spanish explorers to Gran Quivira for almost sixty years. In 1601, Juan de Oñate, the newly appointed governor of New Mexico, again moved by the spirit of Spanish expansion, led seventy picked horsemen on an expedition from the Pecos to the Canadian. He traveled down the Canadian to the center of the Texas Panhandle, turned northeastward to Gran Quivira, and crossed No Man's Land, as Coronado and his men had done before him, although Oñate used a parallel route. In subsequent decades, other conquistadors visited every part of the Southern Plains, making new trails and marking old ones.

By the middle of the eighteenth century, French *voyageurs* and *coureurs de bois* in the Illinois country had learned of these Spanish enterprises and had begun to cross No Man's Land to barter with the Spaniards and with the nomadic Indians. Their heavily laden pack trains of horses and mules were given a welcome in Santa Fé, whose inhabitants were eager to trade Spanish gold and silver for such French goods as balls of wool, beaver hats, cotton and linen cloth, muslin, silk and woolen stockings, scissors, needles, thread, and luxury items. The Spanish governor frowned when he learned that French traders had also sold *escopetas* (guns) to the Comanches at La Jicarilla and that Indians had used them on exposed Spanish settlements at Galisteo and Pecos.

For more than ten years between 1739 and 1752, Peter and Paul Mallet, Pierre Satren, Jean Chapuis, and other Frenchmen engaged in this profitable trade. But during the same period Comanche forays against the Spaniards increased. Governor Tomás Vélez Cachupin decided in 1752 that the late-comers, Chapuis and his traders, had intrigued with the Comanches against the Spaniards. He ordered them imprisoned and their trade goods confiscated. Chapuis confessed that he had expected to pay the cost of his journey from Illinois through the sale of most of his goods to the Spaniards, but he denied that he had hostile motives when he used some goods as presents to the "barbarians" (Comanches). His admission that guns and powder had been given to the Comanches convinced Cachupin that Chapuis and his men were enemies, and French visits ended. Other efforts to continue commercial relations between these two people failed, but the invaders had made one significant contribution: they had pioneered the Santa Fé Trail, an honor, incidentally, which was claimed by Missourians seventy years later.

Until the end of the eighteenth century neither the Spaniards nor the French made attempts to settle the High Plains, of which No Man's Land was a part, although they crossed it many times. In fact, their descriptions range between wide poles. Generally, those who visited No Man's Land in the spring or early summer found the wide, sweeping prairies carpeted with lovely green grass and wild flowers. During this period, No Man's Land was where "Lotus Eaters dreamed their lives away," where the buffalo and the deer grazed to repletion on the succulent grama and bluestem grasses. It was a land "of purling streams and deep, swift rivers of sweet water."

But others who came in late July or August found the prairies brown and parched, a land "of isolation and death," with tantalizing mirages and whirlwinds, like spiraling wraiths dancing in the distance. This was a season when "the burning sun scorches and the blazing winds wither the grass and trees;—where human beings and animals perish of heat and thirst—and were reft of life by the fearful blizzards which swept over the cheerless, treeless prairies in winter."

7

These and other pen-pictures seem antithetical. Yet they were realistically accurate in presenting No Man's Land as a land of violent seasonal changes. No wonder early trappers, traders, and adventurers shunned it in crossing the Plains!

The echoes of *voyageur* footsteps had barely died along the dim No Man's Land trail when Anglo-American explorers came to cross the region after the United States had purchased the Louisiana Territory in 1803. But the Americans were not favorably impressed. They could hardly believe that a desertlike waste of midsummer could change to a verdant paradise in the following spring. In 1806, Zebulon Montgomery Pike traveled up the Arkansas River to the Rockies, passing at points but a short distance north of No Man's Land. He saw all about him great sand dunes. "These vast plains," he said in his report, "may become in time as celebrated as the deserts of Africa." Major Stephen H. Long crossed the same general region fourteen years later and officially named it the "Great American Desert." He felt quite sure that the Great Plains were "wholly unfit for cultivation." He thought the area unsuitable for the white man but admirable for the Indian, since it had enough water, wood, and wild game for the latter's use.

Thus, the theory of the "Great American Desert" was launched. And it was seconded in 1824 when the Woodbridge and Willard geography stated that "from longitude 96 degrees, or the meridian of Council Bluffs, to the Chippewain Mountains, is a desert region four hundred miles in length and breadth, or about sixteen hundred miles in extent."

Anglo-American traders who visited No Man's Land

after Long's expedition, came to understand the region's drastic seasonal changes. William Becknell, Josiah Gregg, and others, with their caravans of cumbrous wagons, spent many days in the land on each trip over the Santa Fé Trail. When they moved south of the Arkansas, to use the Cimarron cutoff, they had to cross No Man's Land, but they seldom tarried, except to repair a broken-down wagon or to camp along a spring-fed stream.

Occasionally they found favorable camp sites. Among these was Willowbar Crossing of the Cimarron, north of present-day Boise City, Oklahoma, but then in the northwestern part of No Man's Land. The crossing was so named for the willows growing along the river bank. Two others were at the Upper Cimarron Springs and at Cold Springs. The latter, also north of Boise City, was enclosed by high banks, which offered protection to the traders' stock at night. At this place, on a sandstone bluff from ten to thirty feet high, traders occasionally inscribed their names, and other wayfarers have followed this practice in the years since.

It was at such a camp site on the Cimarron in the northwestern part of No Man's Land that a caravan and an escort of United States cavalry stopped in June, 1831. The traders had scarcely corralled their wagons when more than one thousand Blackfeet and Gros Ventre Indians rode up, making friendly signs to them, explaining that they were peacefully touring the Southern Plains with their women and children. That night a few of the chiefs and warriors entertained the traders with dances and songs, but the white men watched suspiciously every move and slept little after the red visitors went away.

By daybreak the next morning, the traders hurriedly

left camp for the open prairies of No Man's Land. They now relaxed, believing that they had escaped danger. But presently they met a Comanche war party. All was now confusion. Quickly wagons were corralled and the troops deployed to meet the Indian assault that was not long in coming. Howling like madmen, the Comanche warriors dashed forward, hoping to stampede the horses and to take away plunder. But the traders and troopers repelled the attack and proceeded to Santa Fé.

Josiah Gregg was a member of this caravan. Interested in science, he noted the country's disadvantage, its inclement weather. He wrote that sometimes "storms of hailstones larger than hen's eggs" came with the rain, and that "the violence of the wind is so great that two road-wagons were once capsized by one of the terrible thunder-gusts; the rain at the same time, floating the plain to the depth of several inches." But he also understood the region's advantages. Along the creeks and ravines he found dense thickets of underbrush, matted with green brairs and grapevines, which, with wild currant and plum bushes, were "all bent under their unripe fruit." No Man's Land undoubtedly had possibilities.

The country's wildness, its "towering cliffs, craggy spurs and deep cut crevices," were unforgettable to Gregg. "They become doubly impressive to us," he said, "as we reflected that we were in the very midst of the most savage haunts."

A well-known English physician of this period, Dr. John Charles Beales, who had lived for several years in Mexico and had married a Mexican woman, Doña Dolores Soto, evidently thought better of the country. He and Mexican associates secured a contract from the Mexican state of Texas-Coahuila to colonize a huge tract of land extending from the Rio Grande to a line parallel to, and twenty leagues south of, the Arkansas River (approximately the northern boundary of No Man's Land). In the summer of 1833, Beales dispatched Major A. Le Grand and a party of men from Santa Fé to survey the territory.

The surveyors first established the southeastern corner of the grant at the junction of the thirty-second parallel and the one hundred and second meridian. Then they moved northward, marking "section" after "section." On September 16 they reached the north fork of the Canadian River, and on the next day established the northeastern corner of the grant. "Sep. 17th.—N. along the E. side of section 12," read an entry in Le Grand's field notes. "Today we made twenty-five miles, to the supposed corner of section 12." This point, as located on John Arrowsmith's map used as a frontispiece in William Kennedy's *Texas*, is only a short distance south of the thirty-seventh parallel and east of the present-day Oklahoma Panhandle town of Carthage. From it, the traders went westward, paralleling the Arkansas River.

On September 21, while still in what became officially No Man's Land, the surveyors saw a large party of Indian warriors, who that night drove away the surveyors' horses; but the animals came back to camp the next day. Six days later, in the same vicinity, Le Grand wrote that "about midnight we were attacked by a party of Snake [probably Comanche] Indians." But after a desperate fight the war party was driven off, leaving nine dead warriors. Three of Le Grand's surveyors were killed and one was slightly wounded.

Le Grand's report possibly convinced Beales that he should not risk planting his first colony in so inhospitable a region, for subsequently he located his settlement several hundred miles farther to the southeast, near the junction of Las Moras Creek and the Rio Grande. Some of his colonists had recently come from Europe—England, Ireland, and Germany—and were inexperienced for such a hazardous colonial undertaking. The country was semiarid, densely overgrown by mesquite, chaparral, greasewood, and prickly pear, and was ranged by Comanche war parties. After a year's precarious stay, and after Santa Anna had crossed the Rio Grande to drive all Anglo-Americans from Texas, the colonists abandoned the settlement and scattered to more civilized areas.

For a decade and a half after the Texans had won their independence at San Jacinto, few people visited No Man's Land. Meanwhile, New Mexican *comancheros* had brought heavily laden burros and *carretas* from San Miguel and other outpost towns to trade with the wild Indians; and Missourians had continued to cross the northwestern uplands on their way to Santa Fé. Yet the only permanent occupants of No Man's Land were the Comanches and Kiowas who found here vast numbers of buffalo, deer, and antelope.

But after this lull events presently moved more swiftly. First the federal Congress acted, unintentionally, to set apart No Man's Land. In 1850 it bought Texas' western claims and fixed the northern boundary of its Panhandle at 36 degrees and 30 minutes of north latitude; and in the same year it established New Mexico's eastern boundary at the 103d meridian by establishing the southern boundary of Kansas at the 37th parallel. The western boundary of Indian Territory at the 100th meridian had already been fixed by the Spanish treaty of 1819.

The outbreak of the War Between the States diverted the attention of the American people from the western territories and fixed it on the problems of the conflict which was about to absorb the energy of both sides for the ensuing four years. Thus, No Man's Land remained Indian country for many years to come.

II

"Don't Go Out 'Thar'!"

For more than three hundred years, No Man's Land remained untamed Indian country. Except for occasional Indian camps pitched there in hunting seasons or for trading with the *comancheros*, it was entirely unoccupied. Still, over the land had flown the flags of five nations: Spain (1541–1682, 1763–1800, 1819–1821); France (1682–1763, 1800–1803); Mexico (1821–1836); Texas (1836–1846); and, at last, the United States, after the annexation of Texas in 1846.

By 1860 the white man's roads and trails crisscrossed No Man's Land's grassy plains, and his lucrative prairie commerce continued to pass over the Santa Fé Trail. It was also a profitable trade for the Comanche and Kiowa warriors who attacked the wagon trains along the trail's meanderings below Fort Dodge. During the winter of 1864, Colonel Kit Carson sought to end these raids and led a strong force of federal troops eastward from New Mexico to a large Comanche village near the site of Bent's old trading post in the Texas Panhandle. The village was burned, but the invaders could not remain in the country. Fierce, repeated assaults caused them to retreat, and they succeeded in getting back to New Mexico only after using two field pieces to hold the vengeful Indians at bay.

Carson's near-defeat alarmed General James J. Carlton, the commander of the military district. Carlton feared that unless Comanche and Kiowa attacks on the caravans stopped, traffic over the Santa Fé Trail would be reduced so materially that the Union supply line between New Mexico and St. Louis would be in danger. New Mexico was undermanned and poorly protected, but troops from Fort Union were used to protect the traders. Carlton proposed to establish a fort on the Santa Fé Trail, well within the danger zone, which would give greater protection. The War Department endorsed Carlton's proposal and instructed Colonel Carson "with Major Albert H. Pfeiffer and Company C and L" of his regiment to proceed from Fort Union, about thirty miles north of present-day Las Vegas, New Mexico, to "Cedar Bluffs or Cold Springs on the Cimarron route," to establish the post. Any good site near these places could be used for a location.

Following these instructions, in June, 1865, Carson chose a site on the rocky bluffs of a small stream just off the trail, four or five miles within No Man's Land, east of the New Mexico line. Here he built a quadrangle-type fort, about two hundred feet on each side, which enclosed a cavalry stable, the commissary, the hospital, and tents and dugouts for living quarters for three hundred men. Officers' quarters were built outside the fort.

Lieutenant R. D. Russell, a young officer with Carson, was newly married to Miss Marian Sloan, the twenty-year-old daughter of the Fort Union surgeon. The young bride had asked Carson to permit her to accompany Russell on the first march to the new post site, but Carson advised her to wait. The ever present danger of Indian attack and the arduous work required of young Russell for the beginning of the fort made it inadvisable for her to go with him. Two weeks later, however, after the construction work at the new post was well advanced, Carson sent Russell back to Fort Union for supplies, and Mrs. Russell returned with her husband.

At Fort Nichols, the new post, Mrs. Russell found five other women: the wife of Captain Henderson, two wives of Mexican soldiers (the wives serving as laundresses), and two squaws—who helped her to endure the humdrum of camp life. She spent her time taking short walks, watching the squaws tan the hides of deer brought in by the hunters, and riding horseback occasionally with Major Pfeiffer. She also had to make livable the crude hut which she and her husband occupied. A folding table and a bed, made from a six-foot log, split and laid on the floor, was the only furniture. All cooking was done in Dutch ovens. The commissary supplied her with hardtack, bacon, beans, beef, flour, sugar, and coffee. The diet was supplemented with wild game brought in by the hunters, and occasionally with dried and canned fruit, at two dollars per can.

When Mrs. Russell later wrote of her experiences, she said that the most substantial houses of the post were half-dugouts, with stone for the walls above ground and with supports of logs which were brought in from timber stands eleven miles from the fort. Each of the houses had two dirt-floored rooms, blankets were used for doors, and there was "white cloth over the window frames in place of glass."

Carson occupied a tent, the sides of which were usually rolled up. He lay much of the time on his rough bedstead, "made of four short, forked posts set in the ground with poles across," scanned the encircling prairies and watched for the approach of hostile warriors who never came. He was a wizened, alert little man, "kind and courteous, slow of speech and sparing in conversation," who spoke crude English, often substituting "whar" for "where," and "thar" for "there." He remained at Fort Nichols only a short time; just before he rode away, he warned Mrs. Russell "not to go out 'thar,' " pointing off to the Santa Fé Trail.

Carson was overly cautious, for the post was well guarded. Each morning two pickets were sent out, one two miles west and the other the same distance east, and both were mounted on fast horses. At night sentinels mounted guard near the fort, but no Indians ever attacked the post, although wagon trains only a short distance away suffered raids. The mounted howitzers were fired only once, on July 4, 1865. The post was abandoned in September of the same year and the troops redistributed among the forts in New Mexico.

There is little doubt that Fort Nichols rendered valuable service. Every two weeks the traders brought their wagons to the post, and an escort of soldiers joined the trains for the journey eastward to Fort Dodge or Fort Larned, returning with the west-bound wagons going to Santa Fé. "Captain Strom was the first detailed to go east," remembered Mrs. Russell, "and two weeks later my husband made the trip to Fort Larned where he joined Captain Strom's company and together they made the return trip to Fort Nichols, thirty-two days being required for the journey. On this trip there were over five hundred wagons, drawn by horses, mules and oxen. It was an imposing sight to watch the arrival of this great cavalcade of covered wagons with their massive, clanking wheels, and high bodies, to listen to the cries of the men and the cracking of whips, to observe the 'Major-domo' as he rode up and down the line urging forward the tired animals, and to see about sunset this moving mass as it halted and prepared for the darkness."

Thus ended the first attempt of the white man to occupy No Man's Land. Carson's "don't go out thar" was good advice and would have been given by any experienced frontiersman of his day. For more than two decades white settlers scrupulously stayed away.

Although the Santa Fé Trail was best known, there were other roads crossing No Man's Land. The most frequently used route went east from Santa Fé and reached the South Canadian about the center of the Texas Panhandle. Here it divided. The main road turned southeast to the junction of the Washita and Red rivers, in southern Oklahoma. The other prong of the trail crossed the Beaver River in No Man's Land and stretched north to the Pawnee country, thus following the general route the conquistadors had traveled to Gran Quivira.

Both of these roads were well known to the *comancheros,* who went from San Miguel and Pecos on the east to the Indian country. In 1864, Lieutenant Colonel Franco P. Abreu of the First Infantry of New Mexico Volunteers was informed that San Miguel *comancheros* had returned from the Indian country on the No Man's Land road, driving a "lot of cattle and horses" they had acquired from the Indians. Abreu learned that three thousand Comanches and Kiowas were camped on the Palo Duro Creek.

Along the numerous tributaries of the Beaver and on the river itself were camping sites favored by the Indians. The *comancheros* drove their heavily laden *carretas* to these remote places to engage in trade with the wild Indians for two or three weeks.

Comancheros drove hard bargains and had a reputation of being cunning and ruthless. For ammunition, lead, muskets, pistols, paint, beads, calico, wines, and whiskey, they received in exchange stolen horses, mules, and sometimes white women and children captives. They had no scruples in buying captives, for they could return them to their anxious kin at fancy prices, sometimes for more than one thousand dollars. In one of the lonely canyons of the *Llano Estacado,* the Indians so frequently bartered away captives, separating grief-stricken mothers from their children, sometimes never again to be united, that the *comancheros* named the place *Valle de las Lágrimas* (the Valley of Tears).

During the chaotic years of the Civil War the white men could not defend their own borders, much less occupy No Man's Land. Therefore the Indian nomads were the lords of these prairie marches. No Man's Land was the very heart of their hunting grounds. Buffalo, deer, and antelope drank at the Cimarron and the Beaver and their tributaries, and grazed the fine grama- and buffalo-grass pasture lands on the adjacent prairies. For what else could the Indians ask? It was a region not only abounding in game but also, in the harvest season, in currants, grapes, and plums. Small wonder they fought to retain it. White men had often attempted the region's conquest over more than three centuries, and it yet remained "God's Land, but No Man's."

III

"Why Do You Kill and Not Eat?"

After many decades, the Comanches and Kiowas had adapted themselves to the exacting requirements of living in No Man's Land. They learned to build conical-shaped lodges, pegged down and laced tightly about the lodge poles to withstand the sudden blasts of wind. With the approach of warm August days, when the buffalo moved farther north to greener fields, the Indians, too, left No Man's Land, not to return until the following spring. The Comanches and Kiowas were buffalo Indians. The bison was their commissary. From its hide, the Indians made clothing, bowstrings, robes, and lodge coverings; and they ate its flesh, either raw, jerked (sun-dried), or boiled.

Ten Bears was jealous of Indian rights in No Man's Land, for his Yamparikas most frequently roamed this region. At conferences with federal commissioners, invariably he argued that neither he nor his brother chiefs could cede or sell the land they occupied; the vast prairie was a wardship from the Great Spirit to be held for all the Indian people. They would not dare barter it away, any more than they would agree to sell the soft air and the perpetual water. The Great Spirit had not intended that the white man's cattle and sheep should graze it or that

2 Mule Team with 4 Trail Wagons

Twelve-mule team and four trail wagons just loaded for
No Man's Land at Liberal, Kansas

Burros fitting out in a southwestern Kansas border town for
the trip to No Man's Land

his deep-cutting plow should destroy the grass. "Do not ask us to give up the buffalo for the sheep," he pleaded.

Ten Bears was the product of primitive No Man's Land, and he could not know how fast the white-settler tide was overflowing the Great Plains. No Man's Land would soon become an unoccupied peninsula between the checkerboarded farm country of southwestern Kansas and the cattle area of the Texas Panhandle. As Ten Bears saw it, No Man's Land was suited only to the Indian's opportunistic and strikingly adaptable way of life. He was right to the extent that he and his people could not have lived there in fixed and sedentary groups, since scientific skill, mechanical appliances, and long years of experience were necessary to tame such a land. During his day, unskilled farming techniques could not solve the problems which arose from the region's blizzards, hot winds, droughts, grasshoppers, and remoteness. Perhaps he understood this better than the white man and was content to live a primitive life on the virgin prairie.

The Plains warriors had slain millions of buffalo before white hunters became their competitors. They had killed them not only for tribal use but for the skins which they could barter. They would trade beautifully tanned buffalo robes for guns, ammunition, and whiskey. Fifteen years before the Civil War, John C. Frémont learned that the Indians of the Upper Missouri region had sold 90,000 hides annually for the preceding ten years; and thirty years later, J. A. Allen, a government scientist, estimated that the Indians had killed annually 120,000 buffalo. It is reasonable to suppose that the Comanche and Kiowa hunters were equally successful.

But in spite of these inroads on the great herds, there

were still millions of buffalo grazing the Great Plains in 1865. The white man's opportunities to hunt had been reduced during the war period and the buffalo had multiplied. When General Phil Sheridan's troops crossed No Man's Land to help launch the winter campaign of 1868–69 against the hostile Indians camped along the Washita River, they saw large herds of buffalo. As Sheridan's own column moved south from Fort Dodge, it was compelled, periodically, to march for hours through masses of buffalo, and Sheridan threw out flankers to keep the buffalo from overrunning his wagon train and frightening his mules.

Thomas C. Battey, a Quaker schoolteacher with the Kiowas, saw much the same sight five years later. "As far as the vision extended over the wide spreading expanse of the plains," he wrote, "these shaggy-headed, huge bodied, clumsy and uncouth-looking quadrupeds were running or grazing in all the freedom of their native wildness, in such immense herds as to defy computation. . . . Miles beyond miles were covered with them, while upon close observation, the long level line of the distant horizon proved to be a moving mass of life."

The abundance of these herds was requisite to the Indians' tenure of No Man's Land. During the many years from 1803 to 1867, as long as the great herds grazed the High Plains, the Comanches and Kiowas kept the white men from occupying their country. No Man's Land, particularly, was far removed from the white men's supply bases, and its barren wastes of late summer and winter were on the side of the primitive inhabitants. Mounted on hardy, wiry mustangs that were acclimated, supplied from a "traveling commissary" (the buffalo), and knowing every hidden oasis and water hole, the no-mads wore down the cavalry sent against them, for the troopers had to seek arduously for water and bring with them the heavily laden wagon trains of supplies.

If the buffalo were plentiful, the nomadic Indians felt reasonably secure, although ominous days were ahead. The homeseeker tide sweeping the plains would soon make No Man's Land untenable for the red man. Already, the deep-throated roar of the white man's buffalo guns, which, by 1867, was heard from the Arkansas to the Rio Grande, caused the Indian much concern.

When the warriors went on buffalo hunts, they met white men bent on the same mission. And when an Indian camp was moved, and warriors, women, and children sought other well-known resorts in southwestern Kansas or in western Texas, they saw white farmers plowing the prairie sod or cattlemen tending their herds. This caused the nomads to think seriously about the white man's terms. At Medicine Lodge, Kansas, in October, 1867, the four powerful Southern Plains tribes (Arapahos, Chey-ennes, Comanches, and Kiowas) had already agreed to ex-change their large prairie ranges in Colorado, Kansas, No Man's Land, and Texas for new homes in present-day Oklahoma. But they did not understand that they could not hunt the buffalo and pitch their lodges here and there as in times past.

The Indians attending the Medicine Lodge confer-ence had seen white hunters shoot down the buffalo and leave their carcasses on the prairies to rot. Satanta, the leading Kiowa chief, was angered by this practice. "Why do you kill and not eat?" he asked the white hunters. Nor did he like the idea of living in a house like the white man. "This building homes for us is all nonsense," he expostulated. "Time enough to build us houses when the buffalo are all gone; but tell the Great Father that there are plenty of buffalo yet."

But as months passed, white hunters appeared in the Indian country in increasing numbers, and the buffalo were ruthlessly slaughtered. "Buffalo Bill" (W. F. Cody) was the most celebrated of these invaders.

One of the least-known but perhaps the most important of the buffalo hunts which Cody directed took place while he was a scout for Brevet Brigadier General E. A. Carr, during Sheridan's winter campaign of 1868–69. It followed Lieutenant Colonel George A. Custer's decisive encounter with Black Kettle's band of Cheyennes in the Battle of the Washita, when, utilizing the element of surprise in an attack at dawn, he had destroyed Black Kettle's Cheyenne village, killing 103 Indians and capturing 53 more. However, his own losses were grievous—Major Elliott with nineteen volunteers, while pursuing fugitives beyond the boundaries of the village, had been slain by an overwhelming force of Indians. Sheridan wanted to press his advantage immediately, and since he did not have sufficient forage for all his animals, he ordered Carr to select the strongest horses and mules of Carr's command and start back to Fort Lyon, Colorado. Carr was to go by way of the Palo Duro Creek in No Man's Land to gather in a small force that had been left there when a part of Sheridan's command had marched from Fort Lyon.

When Carr reached the Palo Duro Creek, he decided to rest his command there for a few days, but as there was better grass on San Francisco Creek, eighteen miles away, he moved to that creek.

Shortly after Carr had settled down in his new camp, his thoroughly alarmed surgeon came to him saying that the soldiers were afflicted with scurvy and that unless fresh meat could be found, the men would soon be in a serious condition. Carr sent for Cody at once, told him that it was necessary to procure buffalo meat, since there were no cattle, and asked Cody to pick enough men from the command to make up an immediate hunting party. Cody was willing enough to do this, but the buffalo range was some distance away, and it would probably take fifteen days or more to make a successful hunt. When Carr explained how grave the emergency was, however, Cody consented to go.

Cody picked twenty teamsters, wagons, a wagon-master, and Sergeant Luke Cahill and twenty infantrymen for the hunt; and with this force he started westward, on what he planned would be a long trip. It was bitterly cold, and the depressions and arroyos on the prairies were filled with snow. There was no water, and Cody's men melted snow to quench their thirst; the horses licked and ate the snow.

On the third day, about noon, a buffalo herd was found sooner than Cody had expected. Somewhere in western No Man's Land Cody spied the buffalo and called back to his men that their search was at an end. Quickly, then, he gave his instructions. He had two horses. He would ride one, the wagon-master, the other; and they alone would move forward. The soldiers and wagoners would wait until they heard the firing and then hasten to the herd. Cody instructed the wagon-master to ride a short distance behind as they approached the buffalo. He planned a run for the herd and hoped that a chase of ten miles or more would bring him close enough for a first shot at the animals.

But fortune favored him. Directly in front of the grazing buffalo, a deep arroyo filled with snow gave him an opportunity to use an Indian trick. He placed himself directly opposite the arroyo and the herd, then wheeled and raced toward them. When the buffalo saw him coming, they ran blindly to the brink of the arroyo and plunged one after the other into the deep snow. This permitted Cody to pick off the clumsily struggling brutes with his Springfield rifle until fifty-five of them lay dead.

At last his men had fresh meat, and they excitedly skinned and prepared it, not only for their own use but also for Carr's camp. Even the buffalo heads were put into the wagons, for, the cook explained, these would make good soup.

This first hunt concluded, Cody started the loaded wagons for Carr's camp and resumed the journey with the empty ones. After a short drive, he saw a second herd, and this time he killed the buffalo one by one in sustained races. Still, he was successful in bagging forty-one of them before his two horses were fagged. The next day he found a third herd, from which he killed enough buffalo to fill all the wagons. He had slain on the three hunts more than one hundred buffalo, a spectacular accomplishment! His men had only shared in it by skinning the carcasses and preparing the meat for hauling back to camp. Cody's shoulder, upon which his rifle had rested, was terribly bruised and so swollen after the first hunt that he found it difficult to put on his coat.

On their return to Carr's camp, while the hunters were still four miles away, they were met by Lieutenant

Colonel W. H. Penrose, Carr, "Wild Bill" Hickok, and a number of officers. Emotionally upset, Carr and Penrose shook hands with each man, thanking him for his splendid work in behalf of the troops, for they had been saved from scurvy. Carr excused all the men from guard duty for a month and also said that he would like to give each man double pay if it were in his power to do so. Cody, too, came in for his share of the glory; he was wined and dined by the officers and was the lion of the command.

By 1870 white hunting parties were making great inroads on the buffalo herds. Comanche and Kiowa warriors resented their presence, although they had bartered away the buffalo country. For several years after they had turned to sedentary life, they occasionally hunted the old range, for food given the Indians by federal agents was insufficient. (Satanta complained that the white man's corn hurt his teeth!)

Those Comanches who visited No Man's Land found few buffalo. In great anger, they joined other warriors of the buffalo country to plan war on the whites. Quanah Parker, a Comanche mixed-blood, took the lead in their "talks," and argued that the Great Spirit would protect the warriors in battle if they attacked the buffalo hunters. Even the hunters' guns could not harm them, according to the medicine man.

At Adobe Walls, a fierce attack was made against the whites, but the medicine man's promise failed the warriors, and many of them were killed. Bluecoats came, drove them into the western Texas badlands, and killed many Indians (the Red River War, 1874–1875). Everywhere the war parties met tragic defeat; they were outnumbered and outgunned.

More remote events also conspired to bring swift destruction to the buffalo herds, for tanneries throughout the United States were competing for hides. In 1871, J. Wright Moaar had sold fifty-seven flint hides to a Pennsylvania tannery for experimental purposes, and another consignment of hides had been shipped to England. Tests of the leather were successful, and soon hunters were on the Southern Plains killing to supply tanner demands. A great slaughter began. Within three years, hundreds of hunters, armed with the Sharp's ("Big Fifty") rifle, were slaying tens of thousands of buffalo.

By 1874 merchants with considerable capital were sending out well-organized parties to establish posts to supply hunters and hide-buying stations well within the buffalo country, at Adobe Walls, at Reynolds City, and elsewhere. Reynolds City, a Texas sod town on the Double Mountain Fork of the Brazos, in 1877 had a thriving traffic in flint hides amounting to more than one million dollars annually.

Over roads radiating from the hide-buying centers, long trains of wagons, usually drawn by ox and mule teams, traveled across No Man's Land toward shipping points, at Dodge City, or southward to Fort Worth or other Texas railroad towns. The prairies echoed with the dull boom of the guns carrying on the work of slaughter.

So great was the destruction of the buffalo herds between 1872 and 1874 that 1,378,359 hides, 6,751,200 pounds of buffalo meat, and 32,380,650 pounds of bones were shipped eastward to market over the Santa Fé Railroad. Robert M. Wright stated that he and Charles Rath shipped over 2,000 buffalo hides, 200 cars of hindquarters, and 2 cars of buffalo tongues during the first winter the railroad reached Dodge City; and that others shipped as much. Writing later, General Nelson A. Miles stated that 4,373,730 buffalo had been killed during the first three years of this great slaughter.

Texans became alarmed at this profligate waste and appealed to their legislature to halt it. The legislature promptly responded by considering a regulatory bill. While the matter was under study, General Phil Sheridan was invited to address the joint session of the Texas House and Senate; so forthrightly, without fear or favor, he presented his point of view: "These men, the buffalo hunters, have done in the last two years, and will do more in the next year, to settle the vexed Indian question, than the entire regular army has done in the last thirty years. They are destroying the Indians' commissary; and it is a well-known fact that an army losing its base of supplies is placed at a great disadvantage. Send them powder and lead, if you will; but for the sake of a lasting peace, let them kill, skin, and sell until the buffalo are exterminated. Then your prairies can be covered with speckled cattle, and the festive cowboy, who follows the hunter as a second forerunner of an advanced civilization."

Sheridan was right, although he did not explain why the Indian could not use cattle as a commissary. The passing of the buffalo and the nomad meant that the untamed West must go; and the "festive cowboy" with his "speckled cattle," and telegraph lines, and railroads did become the forerunners of "an advanced civilization."

A few bulls and cows escaped the hunters and wandered back to No Man's Land to become the nucleus of small herds. In the spring of 1886 the carcasses of two buffalo, killed in No Man's Land, were hauled by wagon to Pueblo, Colorado, and sold. In the winter of the same year two European noblemen, Curt and Hans von Totleben, killed three buffalo on the flats of western No Man's Land. Encouraged by this success, they outfitted for a second hunt in the winter of 1887–88 but were caught in an early blizzard and were almost frozen and starved to death before they reached shelter at a cattle ranch.

Four years later another hunter killed a lonely old bull at Cold Springs, in Cimarron County. When in later years Comanches and Kiowas came back to their old hunting grounds, they found no great herds of buffalo. If a heart-sick hunter saw buffalo drinking from a limpid pool in a distant, shimmering mirage, which vanished in the summer's heat as he approached, he must have charged the illusion to the concentration of his mind on what there should have been. No Man's Land was not the same; its life was gone. It was a barren, lonely waste.

So long as the Indians and buffalo occupied No Man's Land, white settlers stayed away. Now that the country was cleared of them both, ranchers and squatters prepared to enter. Just as Sheridan had predicted, within a few years after the Indians and the buffalo were gone, the prairies of No Man's Land were dotted with ranch houses and fine herds of speckled cattle, and some that were not speckled.

From the destruction of the Indians' commissary and one of the greatest manifestations of wild life any continent ever knew, the white settlers reaped an incidental economic gain. When squatters occupied No Man's Land later, they found the prairies covered with bleached buffalo bones. These they gathered and sold to help pay for their subsistence until they could make their first crops.

30

IV

"The Festive Cowboy"

Although the passing of the nomadic Indian and the buffalo from No Man's Land was the end of that region's untamed era, faint traces of the dawn of the pastoral period had appeared earlier.

If anyone should seek a hero for these pre-dawn events, he would find a New Mexican *rico,* Señor Juan Baca of Las Vegas, ideally cast for the role. Juan and Vicente Baca drove 30,000 sheep from New Mexico to a range near Kenton, in western No Man's Land, to claim the fine grama and bluestem grasslands. In the spring of 1864, Juan sold a good lamb and wool crop and was hopeful for the future of this region. He reported its glowing prospects in Las Vegas. Two years later his former neighbors, Juan and Ramón Bernal, joined him, bringing 2,000 sheep. Thus, presently, a sheepherder's empire was in the making, even though the depredations of Indians and wolves were constant.

But a villain, an outlaw named Coe, had entered this region. He had built "Robber's Roost," a stone, fort-like house of thirty-inch walls, under frowning heights of basalt-topped Black Mesa, beside North Carrizo Creek. For a time, Coe and his gang of forty or fifty outlaws were content to plunder wagon trains on the old Santa Fé

Trail and to make occasional raids, while dressed as Indians, on the exposed settlements of Colorado and New Mexico. His fellow outlaws called Coe's attention to the fat sheep, and until February, 1867, he and his gang occasionally took the fattest of the flocks for their own use; but in that month the bandits killed three of Bernal's shepherds and drove off two flocks totaling 3,400 sheep.

Juan Bernal was in despair, for this was a staggering loss. But Ramón volunteered to take two of Juan's shepherds and two of Baca's men and go in pursuit. The thieves had not expected the traditionally timid shepherds to follow them and were leisurely driving the sheep toward the Colorado uplands. After long hours of sustained pursuit, Ramón's party came upon the outlaws, asleep about a campfire. Roughly, the Spaniards awakened and disarmed the outlaws and bound them securely until the next morning. Then the captors took the thieves' camp outfit, horses, and saddles, and returned home, driving the recovered sheep back to the Carrizo and leaving the discomfited ruffians to make their way on foot back to the Roost.

But the shepherds did not stop here. The growing outlaw menace was reported to Lieutenant Colonel William H. Penrose at Fort Lyon, Colorado. That the outlaw problem was soon solved is certain, but just what method was used is still a matter of doubt. Western No Man's Land folklore retells a story that Penrose led troops against the Roost, captured Coe, reduced the fort with a six-inch cannon, and scattered the surviving outlaws to the four winds. But the Guymon *Herald* of April 24, 1913, carried a different version of the affair, which was written by L. A. Allen, a sheriff of eastern Colorado. Allen said that when the news of the outlaw raids reached him, he went to the Carrizo with a company of Colorado state troops. At night the soldiers came to an abandoned adobe hut and found the outlaws sleeping. "We tied our horses a distance away," Allen stated, "and with a revolver in one hand, we crept up to the cabin, burst in the door and took the whole eleven and hanged them to the cottonwood trees along the river bank. Coe was not in the adobe hut. He was at another place some fifteen miles away and we rode there and captured him, and, as there was a big reward for him, we strapped him to a horse and rode with him to the sheriff who put him in jail." Coe escaped from prison but was recaptured a few weeks later and returned to Pueblo, where a mob lynched him.

This account, agreeing for the most part with that of a Union soldier, Luke Cahill, seems more plausible than that of western No Man's Land, although details may have been forgotten with the passing of time. But Allen neglects to say how Robber's Roost was destroyed.

Baca and Bernal remained in undisputed possession of the Carrizo meadows until 1871, and their sheep grew fat and themselves prosperous. They then moved to the Sangre de Cristos. Local tradition explains their departure by revealing that newly arrived cattlemen paid them $21,000 to leave.

Meanwhile the distant Cherokee leaders heard of the invasion of what they conceived to be their domain and sent riders westward to collect a grazing fee similar to that charged the ranchers of the Outlet. For a time the No Man's Land ranchers paid it, since it was nominal. But the Department of the Interior ruled that the Cherokees had no rights in No Man's Land, since it was yet a part of the public domain; and henceforth the ranchers did not honor the demand for a grazing fee.

The famous CCC Ranch, belonging to Vickers, Wells, and Gates, of Tombstone, Arizona, was the largest of the properties located early in No Man's Land. It consisted of twenty-three townships, embracing parts of the Texas Panhandle and spilling over into No Man's Land. There were twenty-eight wells to furnish water for the ranch's 20,000 to 30,000 cattle, and four especially trained men were employed to keep the water flowing. The 101 (not the famous Miller brothers' 101 Ranch), OX, ZH, S-Half Circle, and the Anchor D were other large No Man's Land ranches.

By 1883, according to the late Boss Neff, an early-day cowboy and a citizen of Hooker, Oklahoma, these and other cattle ranches almost completely checkerboarded No Man's Land. The 101 Ranch occupied the Texaquite Creek country, in the far western part of No Man's Land; and the ZH, operated by the Muscatine Cattle Company, was on the south side of the Cimarron. Each ranch ran about 25,000 cattle. Charley Grimmer, with his IB cattle, held the grasslands about twenty miles up the Beaver from the site of present-day Guymon; and the OX outfit was about five miles northeast of the same place, each of these two running from 20,000 to 30,000 cattle. E. C. Dudley's ranch was above Grimmer's; and the Anchor D, or the Arnold brothers' property, stretched along Hackberry Creek. The Hardesty brothers' 20,000 S-Half Circle cattle grazed along Chiquita Creek; and "Old Man" Kramer, with 5,000 to 6,000 cattle, was on Clear Creek, ten miles south of the Jones and Plummer Trail crossing of the Beaver. George and Frank Healy located also on Beaver River, below the mouth of Clear Creek; and Fred Tainter, on Tainter Creek, a tributary of the Cimarron. The YL Ranch, with 10,000 cattle, was on Kiowa Creek, a few miles west of present-day Laverne, and reached from the Cherokee Outlet well into eastern No Man's Land.

It should be remembered that these were only the large ranches. There were others which carried from a few hundred cattle to a few thousand. But there was plenty of room in No Man's Land, and it was not uncommon for a horseman to ride forty or fifty miles without seeing a rancher or squatter.

For the most part the ranchers of No Man's Land were sober men of good intentions, although they were in a region where the only law was of their own making. It is generally conceded that many a killer or outlaw found a refuge in the land and that, following Western custom, no questions were asked about antecedents. Ed Hughes, an early-day cowboy, once said that he was not a fugitive from justice when he came to No Man's Land, but admitted that three of his acquaintances were. "It would be amusing and probably tragic," he added, "were I to name men now living who in No Man's Land took advantage of conditions as they were then."

With the passing of the buffalo and the nomadic Indian, the festive cowboy did arrive with the speckled cattle in No Man's Land, but the cowboy met with more hardship than festivity. Work on the ranch was a grind, and opportunities for social contacts were few. A dance at a distant ranch, where occasionally one or more cowboys dressed in women's clothes to complete the sets; a wedding; a roundup; or an occasional trip to a cattle market or supply-town scarcely relieved the lonely cow-puncher souls from humdrum.

In spite of the sameness, life on the ranch could be exciting and colorful. Danger was ever present in riding a bucking broncho, in handling a stampede, and in braving a blizzard. In 1883 and 1886, blizzards were so bad that cowboys raced with the icy wind to save herds from drifting into the open country and away from protecting bluffs and canyons on their home ranges. At such tasks, feet, hands, noses, and ears froze.

Among present-day No Man's Land ranchers the terrible blizzard of 1883 is well remembered. On a beautiful, late December afternoon the temperature stood at the eighty-degree mark, and a baffling haze, like a blanket, settled on the prairie. Cow ponies tossed their heads uneasily, as if they sensed a pending danger. Nature seemed to stand still, and sound to carry far, as though it were borne on an electric current. A breeze sprang up from the north and quickly changed to a howling gale, driving before it low-racing clouds and occasional rain-squalls. And just as immediately, the rain changed to pelting sleet and blinding snow, which struck in waves of fierce wind. The temperature was below zero by ten o'clock the next morning.

There had been other blizzards, but none like this. On other occasions cattle had drifted with the wind and had found shelter in canyons and draws far from their home ranges, thus causing the ranchers considerable roundup work and delay in driving the cattle back to the home ranches. Because of this, two drift fences had been built to keep the cattle from moving with the wind. The first of these ran west from Camp Supply, partly across

The Hightower family at the OX Ranch on the Beaver

On the old CO Ranch on Sharps Creek at the crossing of the Adobe Walls Trail; picture taken in 1892 by Fred Shore

the Texas Panhandle, through Lipscomb, Ochiltree, Hansford, and Sherman counties; and the second was built parallel to the South Canadian River. In 1883 these fences became death traps.

When the blizzard struck, the cowboys hastily tried to drive the cattle toward well-known home-ranch wind-breaks, but it was so cold that the cattlemen soon abandoned the drifting and freezing brutes and permitted them to go. Numb and beaten by the wind, the cattle hurried southward until they struck the first fence barrier, and there they huddled against it, unsheltered and without feed, until they froze to death. Others, following closely behind them, also beset by the piercing wind, climbed over the frozen bodies, and toppled over the fence to continue a stumbling race to the Canadian River, where the same loss occurred. When the storm had passed, the bodies of tens of thousands of frozen cattle were piled against the entire length of the two fences.

No Man's Land ranchers suffered heavy losses, although those of ample means soon restocked their ranges. But those who were less fortunate, like Tom Connell, tragically gave up and left the country. Tom had started "from scratch" and finally had become owner of a herd of 1,800 cattle. For a time he prospered. No Man's Land had been good to him, and he had bright prospects for the future. When the blizzard came and passed and the warm sunshine returned, and he rode out to see what the storm had left to him, he found alive only a few more than forty of his cattle.

No Man's Land ranchers had not built fences about their holdings, for they knew that they were tenants-at-will and that Department of Interior inspectors could oust them, as the government had removed the cattlemen of Old Oklahoma (the unassigned lands in central Oklahoma). They permitted their cattle to range the prairies, creeks, and draws, wherever they could find grass. Ordinarily, the cattle were not given feed from the time they were born until they were driven to market. Fat beeves were slaughtered right from the range, with nothing to fatten them except prairie grass.

Promiscuous ranging about from hill to valley, stampeding with storms or from other causes, and mixing with other herds caused the cattle sometimes to move far from their home ranges. This made necessary a spring, and sometimes a fall, roundup, to reassemble herds. C. W. Chadwick relates that once he, Jesse Evans, John Steel, and Jack Hardesty, three of his neighboring cattlemen on the Beaver, made three spring roundups in order to clean up that part of No Man's Land which was their range. On a roundup, twenty or twenty-five cowboys often would be employed and many thousands of cattle would be reassembled. Cattle that bore no brands would later be divided among the ranchers and branded, or claimed by those cowmen who could catch and brand them.

Prices were low for even fat stock. The Darlington *Transporter Supplement* of September 11, 1882, quoted contract prices per animal for spring delivery at Kansas City between $10.00 and $12.00 for yearlings, $14.50 to $15.00 for two-year-olds, and as little as $27.00 for a cow and calf.

Spring roundups found the cowboy at his best. Solitary riding the range, day in and day out, brought a yearning for human companionship. Whether he was engaged in line riding, in repairing a fence, or in pulling cattle from bog holes, his was a lonely life; nights at a line rider's camp or out in the open were not "festive" occasions. Necessarily, he enjoyed visiting whenever possible, and he counted the days until he could ride into a distant town or meet other cowmen at roundup time. There, after the day's work was done, he found amusement in a prank, or relaxation in a game of cards; he could listen to the lilting tunes strummed by a clumsy-fingered range rider on a guitar or coaxed by a puncher from a wheezy violin.

At roundup time, even the cook prepared edible food, for he must match his cuisine against that of a cook of another outfit. Such rivalry delighted the hard-working cowboy, for he benefited. Sour-dough biscuits, cooked in a Dutch oven, sizzling steak and potatoes, son-of-a-gun stew, beans, and stewed apples or peaches provided toothsome variety from "sow-belly," sour dough, and molasses that were all too common.

Prairie roundups taught ranchers the value of co-operation, usually under pleasant circumstances. But there were other occasions, when nerves were taut and tempers frayed by vigilance-committee and range-league work, which contained the unpleasant elements of human strife, for there was no other law in No Man's Land.

During the early eighteen eighties, when Texans drove their trail herds across No Man's Land, local ranchers banded together to stop them. Texas cattle, especially those from the Gulf coast, brought ticks, the carriers of a deadly fever which caused the death of hundreds of range cattle. When tick fever first appeared on the central prairies, cattlemen did not know its cause. Some argued that it was transmitted from the hooves of the trail herds; others, that it was a bovine, air-borne infection; but all of them agreed upon immediate and drastic measures to prevent its spread.

Texas Panhandle cattlemen were called together by Charles Goodnight, on December 15, 1880, to consider the new peril; and he and ranchers Cresswell and Williams were named as a committee to devise ways and means to stop the drive of the coast cattle. Goodnight and his committee first asked Governor O. M. Roberts of Texas for help and suggested a quarantine law. The committee felt that quarantine would be effective if a trail were marked, beyond which herds could not range. The Northwestern Texas Stock Raisers' Association had already presented details showing how such a trail should run, and had asked for a fine of five cents a head for each day the trail drivers allowed their cattle to leave the prescribed route. The *Texas Live Stock Journal* argued that controlled driving would work no hardship on the traveling rancher, since other following trail-herders could pick up strays and compensate brand owners after the cattle were sold in a Kansas market.

No Man's Land ranchers were tenants-at-will; consequently, they had no recognized cattlemen's association to represent their interests. Yet they were well schooled in the old "Mayflower concept" of squatters' rights. Earlier they had formed a league for joint action against thieving, brand-burning, and general acts of outlawry, and the self-organized league was used to meet this new peril.

This decision was barely arrived at when a Texan named Moore appeared with a trail herd from Tom Greene County. When Moore reached the Beaver, east of the No Man's Land town of that name, local cattlemen attempted to tell him just what route he should follow from there to Dodge City. But the league members could not agree among themselves and were presently engaged in heated debate. The impatient Moore finally followed a route of his own choosing, a course of action the No Man's Landers bitterly denounced.

The next year Alf Blocker, another Texan, arrived with a herd, and the Kramers told him what route he should take across their range. This angered the Texan, who informed them that he would drive his herd "just where he damned please." A few hours later several leaguers came to his camp and ordered him to conform to the league's wishes about a trail across No Man's Land. "The Hell you say!" Blocker shot back. "I'll make my own trail."

But his flare-up did not help. The leaguers quietly told him that if he deviated from the trail they had named, they would eject him, his outfit, his horses, and his men immediately. Blocker was outnumbered and had no intention of fighting. "By this time," said a contemporary, "Blocker had eaten his dinner and taken his midday siesta, so he passed the morning's conversation as a joke, directed his cook to prepare a meal for his visitors, and with the dinner the last shadow of trouble over the trail passed away."

The local ranchers, however, did not win. The Texans asked the Secretary of the Interior for an opinion and were told that No Man's Land was a part of the public domain and that no organization had a right to impede or control travel over it. After this ruling, the local ranchers abandoned their efforts to regulate trail-driving; they henceforth sought to keep their cattle away from the Texas herds.

The range rider generally was not a rowdy nor an utterly depraved character, but neither was he an "unhusked saint." Long months of semisolitude on the ranch and trail left him with a craving for the excitements of town life, congenial company, and something to do other than herding cattle. Hence, when he entered a wide-open border town of gambling dens and saloons, his pent-up emotions, energies, and cravings would find release in the company of bartenders, gamblers, dance-hall girls, teamsters, claim-jumpers, and other lively but unconventional souls; and there, too, he would drown fatigue, loneliness, and grudges in raw, red liquor. After he had lost his earnings at five-cent ante or stud poker, after he had been denied additional credit by the bartender, and after he had spent the night in raucous celebration, he was ready for anything.

The occasional "tough" gave his hard-working and sober-minded cowboy fellows a bad name. Under the circumstances it is little wonder that the cowboy became a terror to border townsmen. If in his quest for mischief, he rode his horse into saloon after saloon, shot out the lights, broke whiskey bottles or furnishings, or caused the saloon's customers to dash for cover, he did it all because it appealed to his sense of the heroic. He was cock of the walk and boss of the town. Practically every south Kansas border town was pock-marked from pistol fire, and the eighties saw an angry demand for reform from townspeople.

In August, 1883, the editor of the Caldwell *Journal* wrote a stinging criticism of a cowboy raid on Hunnewell, a new border town which had no police protection. Frequent incidents of this nature caused the citizens to appeal to the county sheriff for aid, and immediately that worthy rode into town to look things over. His arrival coincided with that of eight cowboys racing down the street, firing revolvers at random, and dashing here and there to drive pedestrians to cover. Promptly the sheriff took the astonished toughs in tow and rode with them back to Wellington, where the citizens "granted them the privilege of contributing a little of their loose cash which they might otherwise have expended in cartridges for the amusement of the Hunnewell people."

Small wonder that the appetites of even rough men were finally satiated. There were too many boot-hills, too many lonely graves beside the cattle trails. Town marshals and county sheriffs, backed by angry citizens, presently struck to end thieving and murder. C. W. Chadwick wrote a few years ago that he remembered two toughs who hid out on Jesse Evans' ranch on the Beaver, and it was not until they had gone that he learned that they were Peg Leg Dick and the Blue Haired Kid, wanted in Colorado for train robbery. In fact, it was not the custom for No Man's Land ranchers to be too curious about the rightful names of occasional visitors. Peg Leg Dick and the Blue Haired Kid were callous criminals, but there were hundreds of other fugitives who had killed when crazed by whiskey and only then to satisfy the cowboy's code of honor.

The eighteen eighties saw the dawn of better days in the cow country. The angry mutterings of border townsmen had their impact on a thoroughly aroused public opinion. "Cowboy drinking, gambling, and dueling must go" was passed along from border town to border town.

"Sage Brush," an anonymous columnist of the *Cheyenne Transporter* (Darlington, Indian Territory), writing on March 10, 1885, advised the cowboy of this change. He urged him not to throw away his hard-earned wages on the saloon-keepers and gamblers, anyway. Cowboys kept "card sharps" in comfortable circumstances, while some of the range riders were left not only penniless, but with hardly enough clothes to keep warm in winter. Already, "Sage Brush" said, stock associations had outlawed drinking, gambling, and the carrying of revolvers while men were on duty, and the journalist advised the cowboys to accept these innovations.

Another writer for the Kansas City *Live Stock Record* commended New Mexico cattlemen for outlawing the revolver. "It is absurd," he said, "to strap a brace of revolvers and a belt full of cartridges about a young man and expect him to exist any great length of time outside the limits of savage life. Take off his deadly weapons, and it will be easy for him to remain a gentleman, humane in his feelings and practices."

The Texas legislature enacted a law against pistol toting, but the reform movement elsewhere went even further. The manager of the Prairie Cattle Company, whose property was just over the New Mexico line from No Man's Land, drew up rules to govern his cowboys. One stated: "You cannot play cards in camp during the working season and attend to your duties properly. It will not be tolerated. Any employee violating this rule will be subject to discharge." Then followed a warning against abusing the cattle at roundups and on the drive, and against killing either a neighbor's cow or a stray for camp use. "I expect you to have full rations of beef," the ad-

44

monition ran, "but it must be from the company's own cattle."

These were reforms for use in the contiguous states and territories. In No Man's Land the cowboy was still a law unto himself, and he must yet experience cruel, numerous tragedies before he was ready for better days.

The Worst Blizzard

Christmas of 1885, with its accompanying good cheer, presents, dances, parties, and dinners had come to southwestern Kansas and the ranch country of No Man's Land. In some communities, celebrations lasted from Christmas Eve until New Year's Day. Townsmen, settlers, and cowboys alike could truly say, "This is the season for festivities, reunions, and beautiful presents." Roasted turkey, stuffed chicken, cranberry sauce, preserves, pies, and cakes decorated the table of many a Southwestern home, and even the poorest homesteader, in his sod house or shanty, could look at an almanac, if he had one, and say, "Well, 1885 is about gone."

Just north of No Man's Land, at the small Kansas boom town of Surprise, the enterprising citizens enjoyed on New Year's Day a dance which celebrated the building of a new hotel. The twelve ladies and fifty men who attended this "hop" long remembered it because of subsequent events. The dance was unusual in that six-shooters and cartridge belts were not conspicuous and that the "odor of corn juice did not fill the air." One guest said that there was nothing to mar "the pleasure or to terrify the most fastidious tenderfeet." But this could be said only up to midnight, for then the blizzard struck!

Before midnight the west wind changed to the north

and a thirty-five-mile gale brought great gusts of sleet and snow. One man attempted to reach home, but after going a few steps from Dickinson's house, he hurried back to shelter. Seven ladies and twenty-five men found it necessary to stay in Surprise until the blizzard had abated.

Such a large number of guests was too much for Surprise's hotel accommodations and hospitality. The girls were entertained at the Dickinsons', and the men were also given a single room there, but ate their meals at the Hotel Davis. This small room had to serve both as parlor and sleeping apartment, and being cooped up, with no place to go, brought boredom to the storm-bound guests. A few amused themselves by playing poker, and others tried to sleep in all kinds of sitting and lying postures. Tom Nast would have found here the makings of a sketch worthy of a place in any of the illustrated weeklies to which he then contributed.

John Speer of Sherlock, Kansas, wrote perhaps the best account of the blizzard (Topeka *Commonwealth*, January 15, 1886). He said that December 31 dawned beautiful, clear, and warm, and that New Year's Day was much the same. About eight o'clock that evening the wind shifted to the northwest and struck the prairies fiercely, bringing a fine, white cloud of snow.

He did not measure the temperature, but other writers have said that it was from ten to twelve degrees below zero. It became so dark the next day that objects could be seen only at a very short distance. Speer sought to protect his horses by placing them in a barn dugout; but range cattle, driven by the gale, climbed on the barn roof and caved it in. The horses narrowly escaped being crushed and were brought to his sod home for protection.

47

By Tuesday, January 5, the storm lifted, and the settlers resumed their normal life. Wednesday was also a beautiful day. But, again, about eight o'clock in the evening, the wind shifted to the northwest, then the north, and for thirty-six hours such a storm as the oldest inhabitants had never witnessed before howled over the prairies. Prominent objects ten feet away could not be seen.

Speer did his best to protect his brother's horses by placing them on the south side of the house, under the partly caved-in roof of the barn. He put his donkey on the south side of another sod structure, but by morning neither man nor beast could stand against the fury of the storm. The horses had almost frozen to death, and he had to take them into his house to save them. The donkey died before the storm ended, and a horse at the barn was found ten feet under a snow drift. Speer made a manhole in the drift and fed and watered the horse for three days, until it died.

When Speer got out, he found his nearest neighbor, a Mr. Stillwagon, digging dead animals out of a barn. He had lost four horses and nearly a whole herd of cattle. A Mr. Tract, four miles away, had lost a span of mules; and nearly all of Captain Ballinger's cattle, one hundred head, were frozen.

In places the heavy snow was in drifts six feet deep. These drifts were so compact that teams could travel over them, and in many places range cattle had crossed the railroad fences on the snow and had wandered along the track to die. One settler told Speer that he had counted seventy head of dead cattle along and outside the railroad fence, and another settler found four hundred cattle dead within a space of twenty acres under the banks of the Arkansas.

Up until the time Speer wrote the *Commonwealth* article, no trains had gone west since the storm, although two passenger coaches and two cabooses had traveled east, probably to Coolidge. The Santa Fé trainmen, who at the earliest moment had been sent out in additional gangs to clear the track, made little progress. The snowplow was of little use, because of the compactness of the drifts. By Thursday, Speer counted seventy-five hands, feet wrapped in burlap sacks, who had organized at Garden City, and had progressed west of Surprise about twelve miles. Even then the workers could barely stand in the wind.

"I can scarcely illustrate the severity of the storm," Speer said, "better than by telling you that I counted a dozen antelope within twenty rods of my house, and yesterday three came into my door yard, so benumbed by cold and starvation as to almost invade the house. The imagination will pretty accurately convey to all acquainted with their wild, shy habits, the degree of suffering which all flesh is subject to in this exposure."

Speer's game rooster came out of the storm with flying colors. During the storm he had drifted into the "L" of the house near the door, which was covered with three feet of snow. For two days and nights, Speer, his family, and the horse traveled over him and the rooster was counted as dead. Speer's daughter was digging the solid snow out in great chunks with a spade, when she struck feathers and soon heard a cackle. She found that the warmth of the rooster's body had melted a space around him sufficient that he could breathe. His tail was frozen to the snow, and a big chunk of ice came out with him; but as soon as

49

he was freed, he straightened himself up and crowed shrilly.

Elsewhere in southwestern Kansas the storm was equally severe. At Dodge City the velocity of the wind was thirty-five miles per hour. The mercury dipped to ten degrees below zero, and the snow flew so furiously that people in the streets were blinded. Railroad trains and stages were blockaded; telegraph wires were down for mile after mile; connections with the outside world were completely broken; and for four days no trains could get to the town. Three hundred men were employed clearing the railroad tracks between Dodge City and Spareville, a distance of only seventeen miles. In some places the snow was eighteen feet deep. All the passengers of the blockaded trains were entertained at hotels at the expense of the Santa Fé Railroad.

The Fort Supply stage, due at Dodge City on Wednesday, did not arrive until Saturday. The driver said that the blizzard struck when he was in the southern part of Clark County, but fortunately he found a haystack which gave food and partial shelter to his four horses. The driver himself got shelter in an abandoned dugout and remained forty-eight hours without food, water, or fire. Near the dugout lived an old lady and two daughters, who attempted to walk to the home of the old woman's son on an adjoining claim. The daughters perished in the snow, but the mother succeeded in reaching her son's house, more dead than alive. The driver also reported that the suffering among new settlers in eastern No Man's Land, whose houses were mostly sod houses or mere wooden shells, without plaster or lining, was intense. A traveler who came to Dodge City after the blizzard said that a rancher in No Man's Land told him of seeing cattle frozen and standing upright on their feet.

A blizzard survivor facetiously remarked: "If snow has a commercial value by adding fertility to the soil and hard freezing weather insures a bountiful harvest, the destiny of southwestern Kansas is fixed and her success assured beyond doubt." The writer added that Kansas boys had fought with Joe Hooker above the clouds but now were literally enveloped in a cloud.

Fred C. Tracy, the present Beaver County attorney, relates that on the day prior to the blizzard, Englewood citizens were in their shirt sleeves and bragging about the climate in sunny southwestern Kansas. After the storm struck, it was six days before the roads were passable. Tracy had brought a girl to Englewood to attend a New Year's dance, but he could not drive her home for six days. The morning following the storm, young Fred awoke in his father's store to find that it was not yet daylight, but upon investigation he discovered that snow was banked so high on the south side of the store, where the windows were, that no light could enter. Fortunately, however, he could make his way out of the back door, where the fierce wind had swept the ground clean. Fuel became low in Englewood and the residents purchased first fence posts from the lumber yard and then lumber of heavy dimensions. Grocers practically exhausted their stock of flour and were doling out the small amount they had left when a freighter succeeded in getting through from Dodge City with an additional supply.

Young Tracy's father had just completed a sod house on his claim in No Man's Land, near the site of Gate City, and found a refuge there from the cold. But he and others in No Man's Land almost starved before they could get out again to procure food.

The blizzard was at its worst in central and western No Man's Land. In that area, the elevation was more than 3,000 feet, and there was nothing to break the icy wind. The temperature sank to twenty degrees below zero. Naturally, the losses in livestock were tremendous. Boss Neff says that he and his brother had sought a refuge in a dugout on the Cimarron River. Ira built a fire in the fireplace, but the snow covered the house so completely that the chimney could not draw the smoke from the room. The two men nearly suffocated before Ira got his back against the door and forced it open. It was a narrow escape, for young Boss "was past going." "Quite a few people were frozen to death," stated Neff, "and range cattle perished."

A subsequent check showed that every ranch had lost at least half its cattle, and "in some cases as high as three-fourths of their herds." Tracy tells that from a herd of 20,000 cattle, the Kramer brothers, following the storm, rounded up but 2,500. The Parker family settled on a claim near the confluence of the Coon and Kiowa creeks in the spring of 1886, a short distance north of the YL Ranch. At that time, says Ira Parker, "there were hundreds of dead cattle everywhere, which caused such a bad odor that we could hardly escape it at any time." The huge loss was a stunning blow from which many of the cattlemen did not recover.

Even as far south as Waco, Texas, the storm had been without parallel, and losses in cattle were so high the number could not be counted. A blanket of destruction had indeed been thrown over the whole Southern Plains, and to it may be attributed the deaths of many people, the maiming of others, and the general impairment of border development.

The No Man's Land stockman had organized a league to safeguard his herd against outlaws and the Texan's tick-infested cattle. He had tried without success to discourage the incoming "grangers," as he called the farm settlers. He had worked to build up his herds in this cowman's paradise, and had to a large extent succeeded. But he could not fight the blizzard. Thus, the storm of 1886 had a decisive effect on the No Man's Land cattle industry. Many a cowman "pulled stakes, and hung out a forrent sign," and drove what was left of his herd to a more inviting field. Others, however, grimly stayed on, rebuilt their herds, and thereby laid the basis for the present cattle industry of the region.

Land-hungry "nesters" watched with interest this cowman's hegira. And as the ranchers moved out of No Man's Land, they left behind vast, unclaimed prairies. These the nesters quickly occupied, thus beginning a rapid transition in the country—from ranch to farm.

VI

Valley of the Beaver

Visitors to No Man's Land in early days found little encouragement to linger either in summer or in winter. In the summer months, as Ten Bears, the Yamparika, had once said, "there is nothing to break the light of the sun"; and the intense heat smothered the sand dunes, hardy sagebrush, and grasslands. At the other extreme, the region had its terrible blizzards, icy wind, and pelting sleet and snow in winter. Indeed, this was a wild and primitive country, discouraging to him who hoped to make it otherwise.

But seasoned pioneers found here what the occasional visitor could not see. No Man's Land had fine but small streams, nutritious grass, and fertile soil. Water, wood, and grass had been the three requisites for which the homeseekers had looked since earliest times. Here at least were grass and water. What did it matter if there were only groves of cottonwood along the streams and cedar in the sandhills? They could find enough buffalo chips to supply their needs for a fuel.

The Beaver and the Cimarron were the two streams of importance, but the latter only cut across the extreme northeastern and northwestern parts of No Man's Land.

The Beaver helped the region more, since it plowed from west to east entirely across it, except for about fifty miles where the river dipped into the Texas Panhandle, and left its tributaries to water the central part of the area. Pioneer buffalo hunters and cowmen liked the Beaver. It was a fine, clear stream, which ran merrily in a narrow channel. In the deep blue holes, bass, brim, and catfish found feeding places. There was a rapid fall, since the bed dropped from 4,000 feet near the one hundred and third meridian to less than 2,000 feet at Beaver City.

The pioneers also found that many year-round flowing creeks emptied into the Beaver. The streams acted as thirst-quenching life lines for man and beast, and on the tablelands back of these streams were ideal sites for homes and ranches.

Hundreds of camp sites were visited by buffalo hunters and cowmen, but none was so well known as the Jones and Plummer Trail crossing of the Beaver, about ninety miles south of Fort Dodge. This was regarded as a half-way stopping place on the cattle trail between Dodge City and Tascosa and was favored by cowmen, freighters, and all other travelers. Each day, freight caravans, stage-coaches, cattle herds, and horseback riders moved southward or northward over this trail to make it one of the most frequently traveled in the Southwest.

Perhaps freight wagons used it most. Dodge City, on the Santa Fé Railroad, was the principal supply town for the cattle ranches of No Man's Land and the Texas Panhandle; and long bull, mule, and horse trains daily pulled tons of freight to meet their supply needs. Scattered along the Kansas border were many small towns, but they, too, had to freight their goods from Dodge City. The regular freighting price was one cent a mile for one hundred pounds. A sack of flour would cost fifty cents a mile for one hundred pounds, fifty cents extra freighted to Englewood, and seventy-five cents more to Gate City, in No Man's Land. The rates were still higher on perishable goods. The freighter served as groceryman, dry goods merchant, druggist, and cowboy-supply vendor, all in one; and because of his general utility, he was as indispensable before the railroad came, as the explorer, surveyor, rancher, or squatter.

The freighter needed to couple two or three wagons together to haul the loads given him. The first wagon was the largest and was most heavily burdened, but the second also carried a considerable load. Usually, the third wagon, when it was used, contained only the camp equipment and the supplies for the freighter and his teams.

A bull train of three wagons was pulled by twelve to fourteen oxen, yoked in pairs, and driven by a bullwhacker who had no other aid than a long, sharply pointed whip, and perhaps a sharp tongue. If the train was pulled by horses or mules, the driver rode a wheel horse and directed his eight or ten horses or mules with a jerk line running from bit to bit of the horses. Many an old-time freighter was gifted with a superabundance of profanity by which he urged on his teams.

Stretched out on the trail, a caravan of eight or ten of these train-units, each piled high with an assortment of bacon, flour, salt, cases of liquor, canned fruits, and other goods, and covered with bows and partly-drawn wagon sheets, must have presented an interesting picture on these prairies which were so little accustomed to the works of man. In dry weather powdered dust hovered over the laboring men and teams and added to the miseries of long, slow hours on the trail.

Whether the freighter had charge of one, two, or three wagons, he was the master of his train. The lead wagon had a high-lever brake, connected by a rope with the driver's saddle so that he could throw the brake on or off without dismounting. His freight wagon could haul an enormous load. One observer stated that it was not uncommon for a freighter to transport one thousand pounds per mule or horse, in addition to his own supplies. In this way, three wagons coupled together hauled almost as much as a modern railroad car.

The caravan masters viewed with pleasure the prospect of a summer camp of one or two days at the Beaver crossing, for here they could graze and rest their teams and at the same time find hunting and fishing. But there was another reason why they stopped at the Beaver, whether they were traveling northward or southward. Stretching along the north bank of the river were deep sandhills reaching back for two miles, through which the Mexican Arroyo cut its way to the river. The Jones and Plummer Trail followed this arroyo to the Beaver, and for a part of the way the freight teams had firm footing in it; but here and there were stretches of deep sand, through which the wagons had to be drawn singly, and sometimes by double teams. This caused long delays, often of several days, before the caravan units made the draw and reassembled at the Beaver. But the freighter took all these things as expected handicaps, and while idle did not worry about the future, but spent his time in camp playing cards, hunting on the near-by prairies, or fishing in the Beaver.

Jim Lane had much experience on the Jones and Plummer Trail and in freighting for No Man's Land ranches. He would leave Dodge City with two or three heavily laden wagons to be gone for several weeks. Although he was a man of medium height and strength, unassuming, quiet, and sparing of words, when he spoke, others listened. Above all, he was a typical frontiersman, for he loved the outdoors, the broad prairies, the thrill of adventure, and the freedom of the border.

Since Jim personified Western life, the cowmen liked him. He was always welcome at ranches, whether he came to barter or to visit. Thus he prospered in prairie trade and his wagons were known by all cowboys of eastern No Man's Land.

Tired of traveling from ranch to ranch, Jim decided to establish a cowboy's supply store at the Beaver crossing. Early in March, 1880, he and his family brought a large wagon train loaded with cowboy supplies and household goods to the Beaver and pitched camp near a large cottonwood grove on the south bank. Here he had the advantage of a stationary trade with occasional cowboy visitors, and could hunt, fish, and raise a small herd of cattle of his own. No doubt this had been his ambition for the several years he had known about the Beaver country.

Jim built a sod house for his family and store, "a monument to the skill of the frontiersman," wrote a contemporary. It was made of prairie sod, the main structure fourteen by thirty-six feet, with a fourteen by eighteen-feet "L"-shaped addition at one end. The walls were of sod, thick and waterproof, cool in summer and warm in winter. The rafters reached from the walls to a heavy log ridge-pole, and over them Jim laid willow brush, flattening it to form a solid matting. He used this as a base for a layer of sod that was carefully mortared with clay mud. He gathered whitish gypsum mud along the river and used it as plaster for his inside walls. For a short time he improvised coverings for doors and windows, but finally he secured door and window frames and window panes in Dodge City. He used a stove to heat his home, as did other settlers who came to No Man's Land.

Jim's sod house had three rooms: one in which he and his family lived; a second in which he kept for sale a few underclothes, boots, pants, shirts, cards, beer, a poor quality of whiskey, tobacco, and ammunition; and a third, which was used by travelers. The bed in this room consisted of one or two pairs of blankets, depending on the weather, and some buffalo robes. Jim thought it best to furnish buffalo robes, costing only two dollars each in Dodge City, for they were cheaper than blankets.

The coming of mail service and a postmaster brought Jim his first neighbor. Prior to Jim's settling an Illinoisan, an old-time buffalo hunter, Bartholomew Crawford, had built a two-room picket house on Sharp's Creek at the crossing of the old Fort Bascom Trail. At Tarbox, as the place was called, in 1878 Crawford had a post office and a little "road ranch" to supply the needs of cowboys and travelers. During this period, star routes were projected across the region, from Dodge City to Tascosa, and across No Man's Land from east to west, from Camp Supply, Indian Territory, to Springer, New Mexico. "On this route," wrote A. M. McCoy, an early resident of No Man's Land, "one man made one trip through on horseback. Then for a time he would go from Camp Supply up the

Beaver to some of the cattle ranches, loaf a few days and go back. For this service it was claimed that the government was paying one hundred thousand dollars a year."

On April 13, 1883, a post office was established in a sod shanty near Jim's store. Peter T. Reep, the postmaster, distributed the mail to the cowboys and also sold supplies; but Reep could not compete with Jim, so within a short time he bargained away both his postmastership and his stock to his competitor.

Once more Jim was left to his own devices. Cowboys rode into his prairie oasis to quench their thirst and to buy supplies; freighters stopped to renew old times and to unload new goods; and businessmen, adventurers, and homeseekers, passing to and fro by stage, tarried to sample his beer and whiskey. Frequently travelers asked how they could acquire title to No Man's Land claims, and invariably Jim replied that this was a part of the Cherokee Outlet and not under federal land laws. Probably he believed this, and the statement was not made to keep other supply stores out. In 1882 W. A. Starr of Oswego, Kansas, secured a ruling from the Secretary of the Interior that No Man's Land was not a part of the Outlet but was public domain. There was still much good land to be had in Kansas by the homesteaders, however, and the Secretary's ruling caused no great excitement.

It was not until three years later, on October 13, 1885, that the first rush came. On this date a resident of Englewood, Kansas, received a letter from the Commissioner of the Land Office, A. J. Sparks, stating that No Man's Land was subject to squatters' rights. By night the town seethed with excitement, and homesteaders made hasty preparations to start southward. By dawn of the next day, the Kansans had started the first great race for what was to be at a later date Oklahoma land. The region occupied was northeastern No Man's Land, along the Cimarron River. J. H. Abbott, a later resident, stated that among those to establish good claims were Stoner Cole, Ira Hewins, Harry Edwards, George Jones, A. Hoffman, Dr. Littlefield, and "Uncle" Tom Hill. "In fact," he said, "every good piece of land north of the Cimarron in that valley was a claim. Houses, dugouts, and shacks were numerous within a few days."

Wichita boom-town promoters also heard of Sparks' ruling. Ever since 1879, when David L. Payne had launched his invasions of Old Oklahoma to force the federal government to open this country for settlement, Wichita, Kansas, had been "the boomingist of all boom towns," according to one pioneer. After Payne's death in 1884 and after W. L. Couch had assumed the leadership of the Boomer movement, other promotional enterprises had their genesis here. "Out of this stimulation," wrote an early-day observer, "grew the Beaver City Town Company," which hoped to make Beaver City the queen of the prairies. Its officers were N. McClease, president; C. R. Miller, treasurer; William Waddle, local agent; and E. A. Reiman, a former Payne surveyor, civil engineer.

Promptly after its organization, the Beaver City Townsite Company launched its enterprise. On March 6, 1886, Waddle and Reiman, with four assistants, came to Lane's store and announced that, since all this region was subject to homestead entry, they were there to survey a townsite. Jim received them suspiciously. Were these "city slickers" interested in ousting him? They assured him that they were not. In fact, they acknowledged that under squatters' rights he had a valid claim to his 160-acre tract, including the Beaver crossing; but they were willing to promote his interests as well as their own. If he would give up his claim, they would deed him two choice blocks within their proposed city. As this seemed fair enough, Jim accepted their offer, and on the survey plat his blocks were marked "Lane's Reserve."

Meanwhile, the president of the Townsite Company had sent an agent to Washington to secure federal approval for the proposed venture. Agent Waddle showed all comers that he meant business by building himself a sod house of two rooms, one for a grocery and the other for himself and his family; and he remained there until the bubble burst.

The Wichita office had also been busy promoting the city of Beaver, through the columns of Western newspapers and by distributing handbills and advertising matter throughout Kansas. Success was immediate. By horseback, wagon, hack, and buggy the prospectors came, singly, in twos, and in tens. Jim Lane could not begin to furnish accommodations for the daily arrivals; hence, they made their pallets under the great cottonwoods until more comfortable quarters could be secured or built.

Of the hundreds who came, many stayed and wished to buy town lots. Of course the Beaver Townsite Company was willing to sell, but the federal government would not recognize its survey or claims. The company agent was told that No Man's Land was a part of the public domain, but that no court or land office had jurisdiction there. The stunned Townsite Company officials were now at their rope's end. There was nothing else they could do. But the prospectors and the newcomers helped themselves to choice claims so that they would have prior rights when the country was finally opened for settlement.

Jim also prospered. The company had made his store the northwest corner of Douglas Avenue and Main Street, two 100-foot thoroughfares; for a few weeks there were no other stores to break his monopoly in supplying the needs of the new arrivals.

Beaver City, as the new town was called, was much like the average border boom town of the eighties. Throughout the day there could be heard the sound of hammer and saw, the voices of men and women engaged in swapping experiences or in excited bartering, the freighters' calling to their teams, the neighing of horses, the braying of mules, and the usual din of a busy, new, and booming settlement. Every day brought something new. Here and there men worked at the plow and spade, making ready the sod for new houses; freighters arrived from Dodge City with caravans of household goods, groceries, dry goods, and hardware; the stagecoach brought the mail and strangers to stay at George Blake's hotel until they "could get located."

Business houses sprang up on either side of the river bottom and Douglas Avenue. North of Lane's store and across Main Street, D. R. Healy built a livery stable, the indispensable enterprise in any frontier town; and next door to the stable was a long sod dance hall, with an annex for its girls. This establishment was managed by O. P. Bennett and Charley and Pat Tracy, enterprising frontier characters whose developing reputations would stand them in no good stead. Almost directly across Douglas Avenue from the dance hall, Jim Donnelly, a typical, corpulent saloon man of that day, with his red face draped by a heavy mustache, erected a saloon to furnish beverages to the dance-hall patrons and those visiting at the two-story frame Blake Hotel. Near by was also a stock of dry goods in a frame building erected by Addison Mundell and leased to Frank Parmer and Rube Chilcott, whose stock was a wagonload of cowboy supplies they had been unable to sell to cowmen east of the new town.

Other business houses such as groceries, saloons, a hardware store, and a boot-and-saddle shop appeared along Douglas Avenue; residents built their sod houses west of these structures near the site of the present-day Beaver, Meade and Englewood Railroad station, and east of the dance hall, where there was a stately grove of cottonwoods. Here "Doc" Linley and his new Iowa bride "set up housekeeping."

Farmers, or "grangers," as the cowman called them, were no less busy in building dugouts and sod houses and in plowing their fields. In keeping with the frontier spirit, they helped each other to get started in the new land. Whether they were plowing the fields, constructing a dugout in the side of a hill and covering it with brush and sod, or working together in building a sod house, ties of friendship were made through the community labor.

To build a sod house, a smooth layer of the thick turf was plowed; then the sod was chopped into slabs two feet long and a few inches thick. These were laid one upon the other much as a mason places brick to build a wall. No cement was used, for the rain and snow of winter caused the slabs to amalgamate into a solid block of earth. Generally the roof was made much like the one on Jim Lane's house previously described, but occasionally poles were laid across the walls and covered with gunny sacks stretched to form a base for the sod. This, of course, placed a great weight on the roof, which prolonged rains could cave in, sometimes causing the death of dwellers. The floors were earth, packed hard with water and kept clean by sweeping. A few of the sod houses had fireplaces and chimneys, but ordinarily stoves were used, since buffalo chips would burn better in them than in fireplaces. The average house had two windows and one door; but some more luxurious structures had four rooms or more, with board floors and shingle roofs. Although few houses were attractive in appearance, they were far more comfortable than some poorly constructed rural homes of today.

When once the most favorable building sites had been occupied at the river end of Douglas Avenue, the higher ground farther south was chosen for new structures. Indeed, as a rule, business and professional men avoided the river bottom with its saloons, gambling dens, and bawdy houses. Second Street, south of Main, was the line beyond which respectable women seldom went. But from Third Street and Douglas Avenue, where E. E. Eldridge established the *Territorial Advocate,* to Lane's store, there stood a line of substantial buildings, including Thomas Braidwood's hardware store, a lumber yard, and T. A. Garrigues's general merchandise store. Across the avenue from these buildings were others, including Dr. O. G. Chase's two-story building, the upper floor of which was called an opera house, which seldom saw opera but was used principally for dances and public meetings.

Within a period of ninety days from the start of the boom, many substantial business and professional men had come to Beaver. Among these were Dr. J. A. Overstreet, a physician; Dr. J. H. Errett, a physician, and his father-in-law, Rev. R. A. Allen, a Methodist minister; Andrew M. Fenner, E. R. Coffey, and Merrett Magann, grocers; Jake Thomas and O. K. Rogers, druggists; J. H. Alley, with a general store; J. C. Hodge, dry goods; T. P. Braidwood and his son, hardware; J. and R. G. Breckenridge, lumber; T. A. Garrigues, general merchant; Joseph Hunter, cowboy bootmaker; Victor Metzger, builder of a number of rental business houses; and Dr. O. G. Chase, physician, local politician, and business promoter.

Beaver City leaders sponsored a school, for which a sod house was built on the east side of Douglas Avenue. The first term of school, maintained by popular subscription, began in the late fall of 1886 or the early winter of the next year, with Mary Hunter as teacher. In this year, Rev. R. M. Overstreet directed the erection of a Presbyterian church, one of the oldest protestant churches in Oklahoma outside of the land of the Five Civilized Tribes.

Beaver City, the capital of No Man's Land, having sprung up in the valley of the Beaver in less than six months, possessed many signs of immaturity. Bull trains continued to stall in the deep sand dunes of Douglas Avenue until clay was hauled in to make a firm footing; and townsmen had yet to solve the problems of civil government and law enforcement, which also tended to stall in the shifting sands of a migrant population.

VII

A Fight to Survive

By the fall of 1886 around three thousand settlers had come to No Man's Land and six towns had been established, with Beaver as the self-acclaimed capital. This had required numerous business contracts—selling and buying—a general respect for town and country property claims, and the starting of schools, just as in any federal state or territory. There were no legal restraints, no courts, and no land offices on this federal property; still, conduct was regulated. American pioneer history does not record another similar instance.

The No Man's Land pioneer was well informed on the methods of homesteading government land and townsite lots. Rev. Overstreet wrote that the settlers had Kop's land laws and other books of instruction on the subject, so that it was an easy matter to determine every man's rights. By these rules, the settlers could measure sections and quarter-sections of land fairly accurately from the known government township lines, and care in land selection was followed in most cases.

Only through post offices and mail carriers did the federal government carry out its functions in No Man's Land. These came with the settlement of the country.

Gate City, in a fine buffalo and grama grass valley, in northeastern No Man's Land, about fifteen miles south of Englewood, Kansas, was the next town after Beaver to boast of a post office (April 15, 1886). In September, three others—Benton, Blue Grass, and Optima—were established. Benton stood at the mouth of Mexico Creek; Blue Grass, on Kiowa Creek, fifteen miles south of Gate City; and Optima was nine miles northeast of present-day Guymon. And in the extreme northwestern part of No Man's Land, near the Black Mesa, Carrizo (present-day Kenton) furnished mail service for the cowmen by the same date.

Few prospective homesteaders realized the severe handicaps of pioneering in No Man's Land. It was a new country that was so far removed from marts of trade and centers of orderly life that it was extremely attractive for questionable characters. It was free to all and easy of access, and the primitive travel of those days, as in a covered wagon, required no great expense. If an adventurer came from a great distance, he would load all his effects into a railroad car and journey to the nearest point to No Man's Land. Then he would disembark, reload his baggage on a freight or immigrant wagon bound for the land of promise, ready for whatever might open up, with no plans and often not caring about prospects of employment. Under such circumstances, these "floaters" turned to gambling and thieving. To balance this element, there were many others who had come expecting to make new homes by honest toil. Many of these had been deceived by clever promoters who spoke only of the country's many advantages but not of its disadvantages.

In fact, many homesteaders for the first time realized

Jim Lane store and residence at Beaver

The Reverend Overstreet's Presbyterian church at Beaver
—the first church

that they had come to a land beyond the pale of law, where no crime, even murder, could be prosecuted. They were literally on an island 34.5 miles wide and 167 miles long, to which had drifted undesirable flotsam and jetsam from the adjacent states and territories.

At first the cowman welcomed the homesteaders as neighbors. Then the ranchers became alarmed to see the first few immigrants followed by a host of others, who built dugouts and sod houses on 160-acre claims that heretofore had been regarded as cattle range. When a rancher objected, he was told that No Man's Land was public domain and that any homesteader had squatter's rights to a quarter-section of it. The rancher attempted to discourage the granger by telling him that he had been deceived, that this region was too arid for farming. Even the border press, friendly to cattlemen, emphasized the same point, for as early as February 25, 1882, the Darlington, Indian Territory, *Cheyenne Transporter,* warned: "This is not a farming country and those who come with that sole dependence will most assuredly come to grief."

Inevitably ill feeling sprang up between the cowman and the homesteader. There was neither fence nor herd law in No Man's Land, since there was no law of any sort. Consequently, cowmen made no pretense of keeping their cattle out of the settlers' fields.

Those few homesteaders who had crossed over the Kansas line in the early spring of 1885 met with good fortune. The following summer was wet and sod crops did well, for corn sold at fifteen cents per bushel. There was also a fine feed crop, and even though ranchers had to buy large quantities of both corn and forage for their stock, they refused to buy from the nesters. Instead, the cattle were turned loose to graze on the settlers' green fields. When the farmers planted castor beans, to supply a lively market, the cowboys went into the fields at night to pull up the new plants, the ranchers claimed that the beans were poisonous to cattle.

J. H. Abbott, an early-day No Man's Land settler, related an interesting incident of this cowboy-nester rivalry. His neighbor had a fine, growing corn crop and had tried to persuade adjacent ranchers to keep their cattle off of it; the only reply had been laughter. Thoroughly irked, the farmer killed a cow in his field, and a cowboy shot at him as a rejoinder. Then, when the cattle continued to enter his field, he used a long-range rifle, to stay away from cowboy bullets, and killed several cattle and shot at horsemen who approached his claim. The rancher naturally took this seriously, said Abbott, for it was his cattle that the homesteader had killed. Quite disturbed, he came to Abbott and asked him to ride over and remonstrate with his neighbor. "I did not like to take the chance," he said, "so I walked the mile, and got them together peaceably. The next day boys with high-heeled boots were using spades digging post holes, much to their chagrin."

The "Indian scare" was the rancher's favorite trick to rid the country of homesteaders. Kansas border settlers had early borne the brunt of Indian forays, and memories of these bloody experiences were still fresh. Cowmen knew this, too, and more than once had sent word to the settlers that the Indians had broken away from their reservations and were heading for the settlements.

Border Kansans still remembered the scare of September 7, 1882, when Robert N. Wright had written the Kansas Adjutant General from Dodge City that there had been several parties of Indians seen by settlers and freighters on the Beaver, the Cimarron, and Crooked Creek. He reported that Indians had killed a few cattle and had run off some horses, but had committed no other depredations. Noble started for Dodge City immediately and upon arrival found Wright out hunting, apparently not aware of real Indian danger. Noble made inquiry of others and was told that George H. Ford of the Muscatine Cattle Company was probably responsible for the rumor, although Ford denied it. Ford claimed that he had received the report through a system of telephones which connected all the ranches. But Noble was not convinced that the rumor was not a hoax. In his annual report to the governor, he stated that the area embracing southwestern Kansas and No Man's Land was a cowman's paradise, and "as such he [the cowman] ever keeps a watchful eye upon any encroachment. He looks upon the settler as his natural enemy, to be scared and driven away by the use of any means in his power."

Outlaws staged a second Indian scare just as the first homesteaders arrived in northeastern No Man's Land. Adjutant General A. B. Campbell wrote to Governor John A. Martin of Kansas that border settlers had deserted their homes and were fleeing in wild fright and that much suffering would result unless their fears were allayed. He had learned from three independent sources that a band of outlaws, bent on plundering in Comanche and Clark counties, had borrowed this favorite rancher device to get rid of the settlers; he added that the settlers charged that cowboys were responsible nevertheless.

In spite of all the troubles and difficulties that beset the first settlers, homesteaders continued to spill over the

Kansas border into No Man's Land. These hardy people experienced great difficulties and underwent severe tribulations, in common with other American pioneers. Nevertheless, they accepted the risks and courageously battled poverty, drought, hot winds, grasshopper plagues, and countless other adversities.

Long before, the nomadic Indians had warned the white men that the Great Spirit had intended for this country to remain wild; and what the immigrant now saw and experienced caused him to feel that there was a degree of truth in the warning, for even the region itself fought against him. But he already knew dire poverty; he had known it all his life and was conditioned to meet the challenge of No Man's Land. He also found that when the wild buffalo had abandoned this high plateau country to the speckled cattle, they had left behind two means to help the settler in his struggles: buffalo chips and bones.

For a short time the first settlers found cottonwood, walnut, and willows growing along the streams, but the timber was soon cut down and used for building materials and for fuel. Homesteaders could not afford to buy coal, for as a rule they had only money enough to procure bare necessities. Farther north, in Nebraska and the Dakotas, prairie homesteaders had burned grass twists during the winters, but this was a laborious and unsatisfactory expedient. Here in No Man's Land the buffalo had already performed this labor. Millions of buffalo chips were scattered over the prairies, as good for fuel as Nebraska grass. The immigrant's wife was hesitant at first to use the chips, either for cooking or for heating the house. But she finally became reconciled, even to the point of helping gather them up.

The settler also found a ready market for buffalo bones, which were shipped to Eastern companies to be ground into fertilizer to replenish worn-out Southern farms. The cash income was indeed gratifying. Buffalo hunters during the eighteen seventies had unintentionally left this means of a livelihood. Arthur Black of Arnett, Oklahoma, wrote that on one occasion he and two companions traveled from Clear Creek to a point near present-day Gate in search of bones, and that within an area of about forty acres they gathered up three big loads of bones and left as many as they hauled away. They sold them in Liberal, Kansas, for eight dollars a load. "During those times," writes Boss Neff, "I've seen fifty or a hundred skeletons within a radius of a few hundred yards, where a wagon could be loaded in a very short time."

Many times the settler said good-bye to his wife and children not knowing when he would return, and was forced to leave them with little to eat while he was gone. It would sometimes take him two or more days to gather a load of bones, that many more to drive to Dodge City to dispose of them, and as many additional days to return. Abbott stated that if a neighbor had ten dollars to spend, he would usually drive to Dodge City, for it was the only important supply town in southwestern Kansas, and on his trip north he would pick up a wagonload of bones to sell when he reached town.

The housewife was resourceful. While her husband was away, she and the children picked up chips, trapped wild game, and gathered wild plums which grew along near-by creeks. Yet the dreary wait on rainy or cold days for the return of the husband taxed her. If her "soddy" leaked during a long spring rain, or if she and her children were blanketed by stifling heat, without the advantage of shade, or if she could see nothing but the monotonous level plains, life was not pleasant.

Many a sensitive woman, formerly accustomed to the conveniences and society of an orderly community in Kansas or elsewhere, found the silent plains of No Man's Land hardly bearable. Among the manuscripts of a Western historical collection is the graphic portrayal, anonymously written, of the experiences of such a woman, whom we shall call Mary Brown.[1]

Mary and her husband John lived on a No Man's Land ranch. There was neither doctor nor schoolhouse in the community, for there were only three families with children. Mary taught her own two small boys; her neighbor's three children were too young to go to school.

Mary's husband was away from home day after day, riding the range and attending ranch chores. During these periods she would go about her work without a word to anyone but her youngsters. There was something about the atmosphere of No Man's Land's broad, bare tableland that made her silent—bursting with a sense of freedom and yet yearning for the bond of companionship.

In the evening, after Mary had read her boys to sleep, the dead, smothered silence of the plains was broken only by the barking of the coyotes. A lone coyote would call to its mate; and its keen howl, punctuated with short, sharp, staccato barks, would be answered quickly from another direction. For perhaps an hour the wild duet would keep up, making it seem as if there were a pack of wolves around the house. Mary knew that there were but

[1] The narrative is filed as "1. Mr. Bruner," in the F. S. Barde Collection, Oklahoma Historical Library, Oklahoma City.

two coyotes, and she knew that they could do no harm to her children; nevertheless, she hurried to bed and drew the blankets over her head to keep out the eerie sounds.

Two days were required for John to go to town to buy groceries and supplies and trail them slowly home. On days when he planned to go, the family arose at four o'clock in the morning so that he might get an early start, and long before sunup he was on his way with the wagon. When the afternoon sun began to sink low on the following day, Mary and the children invariably started listening for John's return, although they knew that he could not reach home before dark. Sometimes in the night stillness they could hear the heavy rattling of the wagon wheels while they were yet miles away.

At last the wagon drew into the bare, wind-blown yard, and the bundles and the mail were unloaded and taken into the house. Packages were opened, the children's candy was distributed, the news of the town related and discussed, and the mail laid carefully aside to be read at leisure. Mary later recalled how she and her husband sorted the papers so that they could read them in consecutive order. If any magazines came, too, there was added excitement, and the children demanded a story read immediately.

According to Mary's account, there were three rooms to her house—not many to keep clean, but there were also the cooking, the washing and ironing, and plenty of other work. Sometimes her neighbor, who did not have as many conveniences as Mary, came to spend the day with her, and the two women would talk for hours, but they seldom discussed their trials. Then there were times when Mary did not see another woman's face for six months.

Sometimes the deadly loneliness of the afternoon beat into Mary's brain until she wanted to run out on the little slope north of her house and shake her fists and scream at the monotonous beating of the steady wind. At sunset there was only the sound of the sleepy chattering of a belated prairie chicken hurrying home or a shrill chirp from a disturbed cricket. There were no birds, for there were no trees. It seemed to Mary that a dear friend was departing with the sun. The dark was terrifying. At times like this Mary wished desperately to exchange confidences with another woman.

Mary tells of staying at the ranch once for two days and nights all alone when John had taken the boys to town with him. As they were returning, a swift rainstorm, with crashing thunder and terrifying lightning, blew up; and the downpour swelled the creeks and river so much that they could not get across. On the high tableland of No Man's Land, storms seemed to settle down on the prairie. The keen, clear air acted as a medium for the lightning to play vicious pranks. Just the week before, Mary had heard the story of a father's returning from the branding camp to find his three small boys dead, killed by a freak stroke of lightning. When her own family failed to return when expected, her imagination conjured up fearful scenes that were not allayed during the two nights the storm raged. The vivid glare of the lightning played continually, accompanied by splitting and crackling sounds. The thunder beat upon her ears in deafening crashes that seemed to bring the very dome of Heaven about her head. She walked the floor those two nights and without any doubt learned the real meaning of terror and loneliness.

When her neighbor's baby was born, there was no doctor. Doctors did not like to take the long, rough rides into the country, and it took the better part of a day to bring them. The husband was trying to wrap the newly born baby in a flannel shawl when Mary arrived. The new parents looked upon their plight philosophically.

"If it is all right, then we can get along without a doctor," the husband explained, "and if it isn't, then we couldn't get a doctor anyhow."

At another time Mary had diphtheria when a terrific blizzard prevented anyone's getting to town. At last a cowboy was sent. Mary told him to bring her four-grain quinine capsules and potash to gargle her throat. But the cowboy became confused with these instructions; he returned with empty four-grain capsules and a can of lye. "But," Mary added, "we all lived through it."

In all these experiences, Mary fought mental and spiritual battles more rigorous than any against poverty. And Marys were legion in No Man's Land, some of them also struggling against poverty. There were those who met defeat and returned to their former homes; others remained, mentally tortured, buffeted, and beaten, until they adapted themselves to this raw frontier.

How the No Man's Land mother cared for the needs of a large family—and most families were large—is still a mystery. Women economized and resorted to unusual ingenuity. Threadbare garments were made over into dresses, shirts, coats, and trousers for the children or woven into rugs and carpets. Flour sacks supplied material for making children's underwear. George M. Hoover of Dodge City sold a brand of flour called "Old Gold"; high wind did a good advertising job for the flour by exposing a child's posterior with its flour-sacking panties.

The average family had only a slender income. If it could buy salt pork, flour, meal, and occasionally dried fruit, it was well provided. "One day a boy stopped at my house," wrote Arthur N. Howe, "and seeing that I had rice, said, 'You got rice? You must be rich.' " Howe wrote of the ingenuity of his own wife, who learned to prepare the wild plums for future use. She would run plums through a colander to remove the seeds, after which she would flatten out and dry the pulp to produce what was called "plum leather." When it was soaked and stewed in sugar, it made an excellent sauce.

But during the periods of drought and hot winds, when there was little to add to the bone-gatherer's income, his family fared on a diet of bread and flour gravy, with some wild game. Fortunately, game and fish were plentiful during the first few years. J. H. Abbott and a traveling companion approached a sod house near Ivanhoe on one occasion to ask for food. "My man started for Dodge yesterday," the housewife replied, "and we haven't a thing but milk and plenty of mush, but not a bit of salt. If you will eat mush and milk, all right." The two hungry men were glad to get it.

In the summer, prairie chickens, quail, plover, and curlews were everywhere, and in the fall and winter they were joined by great flocks of wild ducks and geese. There were only a few buffalo left in the rugged hill country of western No Man's Land in 1886, and they were hard to kill. But if the settler was a skillful hunter, he could usually bring home an antelope or a deer.

As No Man's Land population increased, wild game

became scarce and the settler had to travel many miles from home to supply his table. Arthur Black stated that one winter he and two neighbors traveled as far as the Washita River country, in what is now the western part of Roger Mills County, Oklahoma. There they found countless numbers of fat prairie chickens feeding on an abundant growth of acorns, and in three days he and his companions shot five hundred birds and several deer and antelope. "We had all we could haul," he wrote, "so struck out for Canadian, Texas. At Canadian, we shipped this game, which brought us $160.00." Howe also told of a similar success. He hunted in the blackjack country south of present-day Alva, Oklahoma. Eagle Creek was covered with a thick coat of ice, but he cut holes through it, made a seine of a gunny sack and almost filled a wagon box with fish, which with venison and wild turkeys he took to Kiowa, Kansas, "and overstocked the market."

Mustang hunting was a novel way of earning a living. Mustangs were wild horses, the progenitors of which dated back to the time of the Spanish conquistadors. From time to time other horses escaped and joined early herds, so that by the eighteen eighties a wild-horse herd represented many mixtures of strains and such colors as roans, bays, sorrels, whites, and grays. The mustang was fleet of foot and his speed was his chief defense against hunters, but when cornered or caught, he fought viciously, both with his hooves and his teeth. Since it was difficult for a horseman to overtake the speedy mustang if he had a few hundreds yards advantage, the horse found the wide prairies of No Man's Land ideally suited to his peculiar habits. Invariably, a mustang herd was directed by a stallion, who kept a sharp lookout for an enemy. As a rule mustangs grazed on the open prairie during the day and visited the creeks or water holes early in the morning or late in the evening.

Hunters discovered this habit and would lie in wait for the horses at watering places. The mustangs were not disturbed until they had drunk their fill, so that their paunches were distended with water and their speed reduced. Riders would then dash among the wild horses and lasso the animals they desired.

Boss Neff tells of his own experience in hunting wild horses. He had left a ranch on Chiquita Creek and was riding toward his and his brother Ira's ranch on the Palo Duro, fifteen miles distant. When he arrived at Cottonwood Creek, where there were some pools of water in a deep draw, he came within two hundred feet of more than thirty mustangs. "They no doubt had been there long enough to get full of water," Neff said, "as their range was out east of this water and up on the high plains. It was the usual custom for mustang or antelope, when they did come down into the hills for water, to get their fill and then get back pronto to the flats, where they could see an enemy from afar.

"I could readily see that the mustangs were very much frightened, so I put spurs to old Fay and by the time I rode among them I had my rope and loop in position to catch one of them. Naturally, I knew the proper thing to do was to catch a young one, for a full-grown mustang on the end of my rope, by myself, would be a real problem. In fact, I had lost a good rope a few weeks before that, when I roped a full-grown mustang out on the head of the Palo Duro.

"Now in this fleeing herd was a beautiful yearling

strawberry roan. He was running near and beside a bay mare and from the resemblance of their mane, I knew the bay was his mother. There also was a blue roan stallion in the herd that I had every reason to believe was the sire of the yearling. I flung out my lasso, and the strawberry roan was mine. One end of the rope was tied hard and fast to the horn of my saddle. In about a minute I had him jerked down and had one foot on his neck and his top front foot was secure in my hand. Soon as I got enough slack in the rope, I made a half-hitch around my hands, so now he could not choke." Neff later tamed "Red," as he called the colt, by yoking him with "Socrates," his burro, and Red grew into a valuable cow horse.

The most unique way to capture mustangs was literally to run or walk them down, a method used almost exclusively by professional No Man's Land hunters. In writing of these early days, James F. Beecham states that a herd of about twenty-five mustangs ranged within the vicinity of his claim. Finally the horses were caught by a relay system. The first riders ran the herd eighteen or twenty miles, trying to keep the horses away from feed and water. Then other horsemen relieved those who had started the chase, the wild horses usually doubling back to their old grazing ground where fresh hunters waited. After several days of this maneuvering, each day the men getting a little closer, the mustangs were completely exhausted and the hunters were able to rope and side-line them. (To side-line a horse was to tie his fore leg to his hind leg on the same side.)

Jim England remembers a similar hunt. He tells that while following a trail herd of cattle through No Man's Land, two of his Mexican riders decided to go mustang hunting. They found a bunch of mustangs about five miles south of the Beaver River and started to walk them down. After the third day they became impatient and changed tactics. They shoved the tired mustangs into a small, deep canyon and then dashed into the herd with ropes ready to hurl. Each man roped stallions about four years old, and side-lined them after a hard tussle. Before they had reached the end of the trail, the two horses were broken enough so that the wrangler could handle them without side-lining them.

Mustangs did not command the price of tame horses on the market. Ordinarily stallions and mares remained wild through life, biting and kicking anyone who came near them, and for this reason only experienced horsemen could handle them. But young animals could be tamed and become as valuable as domesticated horses. In truth, wild-horse hunting was not a lucrative business, and as a rule the hunters were more interested in the excitement of the chase than they were in profit.

To whatever the No Man's Land settler turned his hands—selling bones, hunting wild game, farming, or mustanging—he was faced with the same desperate fight to stay in the country. No Man's Land offered only loneliness, poverty, and hard work. If the settler did get more, he had to resort to skill and resourcefulness to overcome the handicaps of the country.

VIII

"Shake Them Feet"

Dr. O. G. Chase of No Man's Land once remarked, "We have to keep the women contented." That was his way of saying that social functions were essential.

The settler and his family seized every opportunity to attend socials, for they relieved the tedium of border life. All kinds of gatherings—religious services, parties, dances, and picnics—were popular. No Man's Land cowboys thought nothing of riding from fifty to one hundred miles to attend these affairs, and settlers came in wagons with the whole family. No invitations were needed, for as a matter of course all were invited.

No Man's Land ranchers and cowboys did not welcome the coming of nesters, but they enthusiastically approved any increase in the female population, especially if a new arrival were a pretty girl. In one western No Man's Land community, before the nesters had begun to arrive, there had been only two women: one, the wife of the rancher; the other, a visiting young lady, to whom an ardent cowboy proposed marriage many times without success. Each rejection only seemed to encourage him to make another proposal.

But if marks of gallantry, and ultimately a husband,

were the rewards of a woman's waiting in No Man's Land, the male tenderfoot had a less pleasing experience. Not uncommonly an obliging cowboy roped from the remuda his "favorite saddle horse," insisting that the tenderfoot ride him for the day; and if the newcomer accepted the unselfish proposal, he was assured an exciting and hopeless struggle to stay in his saddle. Or, if all the ranch hands went with him on a midnight snipe hunt and generously allowed him to hold the sack into which the birds were to be driven, he had to endure fruitless hours of waiting for the elusive birds. However, the cowboy's favorite "entertainment" of his visitor was the card game which ended in an angry, although faked, row, during which players leaped to their feet, drew their revolvers, and fired in all the safe directions, while the tenderfoot was making for cover.

After many days of hard and lonely work on the ranch, the cowboys of eastern No Man's Land rode into Beaver on Saturday and tied their horses in front of Jim Lane's store, or later, when it was built, Donnelly's Saloon, and went straight for a few drinks of whiskey. Then, fired with the liquor, they were ready for "fun," to be furnished preferably by others, but by themselves if no other eligible person were present. They had great respect for a cowboy who could "hold his likker"; but if a drinker became too boisterous and quarrelsome, he could be given the "rawhide treatment." That is, the fun-makers lashed a rawhide to the horn of a saddle and placed the inebriate on it; then they gave him a wild, reckless ride over town. If the drunk clung to his bouncing "dream carpet," well and good; but if he fell off, he was unceremoniously dumped into a hole, the rawhide thrown over

A housewife gathers buffalo chips on the plains

An early-day camp in the Kenton country

him, and he was covered with sand. If he still did not arouse from his drunkenness, he was buried deeper and a mock funeral was performed over his grave. Sometimes the victim was almost suffocated before he was rescued.

Often a certain No Man's Land ranch foreman slept off his drunks on a saloon counter in Beaver, and his obliging cowboy friends just as often carried him to the sidewalk at closing time to leave him for the inspection of all who passed. But one night when it was raining, they decided to put him up for the night. They unsaddled and hobbled his horse, and carried the sleeper upstairs where some coffins had been stored. There they placed him in a coffin, propped up other coffins about him, hung up a shaded lantern, and left. The sleeper awoke at daybreak to be confronted with the macabre scene. He said later that he was sure the end of time had come and he was being resurrected.

Usually, when the cowboys came to Beaver, they celebrated their entrance into town by firing their revolvers promiscuously. When they reached the brow of the low hill south of Beaver or when they crossed the river to the north, they began their gunplay. Then they spurred their horses into a run and with wild yells and "exploding cartridges made the welkin ring." Their immediate destination was the saloon, where they invited the habitual hangers-on, and usually there were several, to "belly up" to the bar. And after "tanking up," having no more pleasing way of working off their hilarity, they sometimes went out on the street and drove everybody to cover by shooting their revolvers in all directions. "Hundreds of bullets were sent flying about the streets every day and night, and the fronts of all the buildings that were standing in those days are cut and bored through in many places by the deadly missiles. It is a matter of which the Beaver City man always boasts, however, that nobody was ever accidentally shot in that town."

It was not until the Thompson and Tracy dance hall was built that a man was shot purposely. Richard Roberts (alias Dick Davis) came to Beaver from Tascosa in August, 1886, bringing with him two girls for the dance hall. Dick was "one of the Wild West Show cowboys, with long hair and no end of fancy trimmings to his clothes and swagger to his gait," who greatly annoyed the local cowboys. He stayed around town for two or three weeks, boasting of his exploits to all who would listen, and one night while standing on the west side of Douglas Avenue, opposite the dance hall, he again told his cowboy audience "how great he was."

"Shoot the jaw!" said a disgusted listener.

The invitation did not have to be repeated. A half-drunk bystander obeyed the command literally. "There was the flash of a revolver held by Soap Reed, also of Tascosa, and a 44-calibre bullet crashed through both sides of Roberts' lower jaw. The bone was splintered into nearly a hundred pieces, and every tooth but one on each side was knocked out of his mouth and fell on the ground."

For a moment Roberts stood numbed with fright and pain. Then he clasped his hands to his face mumbling, "God! I'm shot!" and, fainting, crumpled to the ground.

Bystanders took the wounded man into Donnelly's saloon and sent for Dr. J. A. Overstreet, Beaver's first physician, who carefully picked out the splintered bones and treated the wound.

The victim had no recourse; there were no peace officers, no courts, and no law to try the gunman or mete out justice.

But those who had witnessed the shooting sympathized with the sufferer. While he was recovering, during a period of three months, his expenses were paid by Beaver citizens; but he left town without thanking them. Indeed, he returned to Beaver later, jumped the claim of Widow Poggenberg, and the local vigilance committee tried him in court and ordered him to leave. This he did, with the committee in hot pursuit, for he had stolen two horses! He escaped and later joined a gang of horse thieves in Squaw Canyon, near Rabbit Ear Mountain, in western No Man's Land.

A dance was No Man's Land's most popular event, and the most gala occasions were on holidays. Perhaps the most celebrated dance of early Beaver was the one held on Christmas Eve, 1888, an event that had been looked forward to and prepared for since the ball on Thanksgiving night. To the present-day reader, this dance may seem of no great importance, for it was like many another held along the border; but to No Man's Land settlers it was the social occasion of the year, more important than the local roundup, a meeting of the vigilance committee, or any other event.

The Beaver *Territorial Advocate,* for several issues, said J. R. Spears, the *New York Sun* reporter, had carried this sentence: "Gentlemen will attend at the cloak room and deposit their hats, etc." *"Et cetera"* meant six-shooters. Only the cloakroom guardian was permitted to carry a six-shooter—he needed it to enforce the rule that no one enter the dance hall with a weapon.

Spears' description of the attire of both the men and the women who attended is worth quoting. "Evening dress in No Man's Land is different from what it is in New York," he began. The ladies wore dresses cut high in the neck, with no train, and the material varied from expensive silk to inexpensive calico. Calico predominated. "The gentlemen, as a rule, wore saque coats, but some of them left coats and waistcoats in the cloak room with their broadbrimmed hats and revolvers. All wore high-heeled boots, and a few of the more dudish among them had their boots blacked. As a rule, the lower ends of their trousers were tucked into their boot tops."

As was generally the custom at No Man's Land dances, the music was furnished gratuitously by locals. George Blake, the hotel owner, led with the violin, and Dr. J. R. Linley and Rube Chilcott played second fiddle, with Mrs. Blake and Miss Birdie Easter presiding alternately at the organ. "It was a matter of regret among the gentlemen that no one else could play," said the visitor, "for both organists were charming young women and needed for the dance, although Mrs. Oliver McClung, whose picture once adorned a page of the *National Detective Review,* was generally conceded to be the most popular woman on the floor because of her figure and bearing, as well as her features."

Spears said that "As the gentlemen passed the cloak room each received a number. This was to prevent trouble on the ball room floor. In announcing a square dance, the floor manager, Oliver McClung, invariably said something like this: 'Pardners for a quadrille: Nos. 1, 2, 3, 4, 5, 6, 7, 8, 9, 10, 11, 12,'

"There was room for three sets on the floor, and the

numbers were called in regular succession, so that no one of the fifty-nine gentlemen present could dance more frequently than any one else. There was no restriction on the ladies, of course, and they danced in proportion to their popularity. In justice to No Man's Land gallantry it should be said that there seldom were any wallflowers.

"When a dance was called the gentlemen 'rustled' for their partners and took their places on the floor in the order in which their numbers were announced. Then each stood about in his place and rested his weight first on one foot and then on the other, and looked frequently toward the music stand as if impatient to begin. The ladies settled their skirts and touched up the frizzes and back hair, while the fiddlers gave a few preliminary saws on their strings to make sure that their instruments were in tune.

" 'Honners to yer pardners,' then came the call.

"There was that about the movements of the dancers, especially the gentlemen in shirt sleeves and with trousers tucked in the tops of their high-heeled boots, which the word spriteliness scarcely describes. Even the sod wall, two feet thick, trembled particularly when Farley shouted, 'Shake them feet,' meaning thereby, 'Balance all.' "

In the issue of the *National Detective Review* that carried the picture of the McClungs, which Marshal Addison Mundell called to Spears' attention, appeared this notice:

$50 REWARD

For the location of McClung and wife. Were at Medicine Lodge, Kansas, on July 24, 1888. Noted dead beats.

The dance of which Spears wrote was attended by people from as far away as forty to sixty miles. A stage load of a dozen or more persons had come from Meade Center, Kansas.

A Christmas Eve entertainment for the children and those few men and women who would not attend the dance was given at the Presbyterian church. There were carols and recitations, and presents were given to the children. But the program was short. The superintendent of the Sunday School, a Mr. Breckenridge, announced that the exercises were to be short so that all who cared to could attend the dance.

John Dale, a Missourian, loaded his wife and twelve children into wagons and came to No Man's Land during this time when young ladies were much in demand at dances. Fortunately, Dale had nine girls, some of whom were old enough to attend dances. The news of Dale's coming was heralded abroad, and the cowboys arranged a dance to welcome the new arrivals, but they neglected to inform the Dale girls of the "shindig," thinking that the girls would follow custom and come without invitation. But the young ladies, tired from their journey and un- aware of what was expected of them, went to bed early. The cowboys anxiously waited for their guests to arrive, so that they could look them over; but when, to the hosts' deep chagrin, Dale's girls did not come, it was concluded that the new girls were "stuck up" and needed a welcome as only cowboys could give.

The Dale family were sleeping peacefully when they were suddenly brought bolt upright in bed by the firing of pistols. The cowboys were riding around the house, shooting and yelling like wild Comanches. The girls tried to get their father to go out and stop them; but he wisely did nothing, and told his daughters that the riders would go away after a while. And as he had said, they soon tired of their demonstration and left. Later, when the cowboys became better acquainted with the Dales and discovered why the girls had not attended the dance, they became "nice and friendly."

Benton became the favorite place for public dances. It boasted a general store, a drug store, a saloon, a hotel, and a livery stable, and could therefore entertain all guests. The hotel served supper, usually cove oysters, to those who came, and the dances started early in the evening and lasted till dawn. Fred C. Tracy says that the town had a reputation for sobriety, and that, unlike Gate City and Neutral City, two small sod towns, it was never "inflicted by so-called bad men," although an occasional dancer might get drunk, "shoot in the air and howl."

Dances were also held in homes, to which whole families came. Arthur M. Howe said that on one occasion he saw several young mothers give a few drops of laudanum to small children to get them to sleep and then later give coffee to rouse them. The average room of a home would accommodate only one set in a square dance. When the dust became too thick from much pounding of the dancers, water was sprinkled on the dirt floor, and the dance went on.

Tracy says that Benton was the first to stage a roping match, the forerunner of the rodeo, in which the contestants lassoed steers and not young calves. The occasion was widely advertised and Wichita newspaper reporters attended, excitedly watching every event and moving about among the crowd. Benton citizens were eager to read the promised account of their holiday, but for some unknown reason the story never appeared in the newspapers.

During the course of the roping match, a drunk man entered the Benton saloon, where a card game was being played and where the bartender was serving drinks. He announced to all that he was a bad man, knocked down a stovepipe with his revolver, and threatened all who might doubt his claims. But those within the room ignored him, for the card players continued their game and the bartender his serving. Seeing that no one took notice of his "heroic demonstrations," the crestfallen and self-acclaimed bad man at last strode from the saloon.

Picnics and pony races were other lively social events in eastern No Man's Land, and farther west the settlers took part in the Spanish *dia de fiesta*. Elm Grove on Kiowa Creek, near the present Highway 270 crossing, was a popular picnic site in the eastern part of the Strip; and farther west, Frisco Creek, Everett Mitchell's on the Palo Duro, and Bill Caples' on Hackberry Creek were other sites.

On horseback and in wagons, buggies, and hacks, people would come from distant homes to attend social gatherings. Some of them traveled so far that it required one day to come and another to return; but since most of these outings lasted for three days, a late arrival could spend at least one day and two nights at the picnic.

During the day at these gala affairs there were horse racing and other forms of contests, speaking, and visiting. Here lasting friendships were formed. At night, while the elders sat grouped in conversation, the boys and girls danced to such tunes as "Cotton-Eye Joe," "Saddle Old

Spike I Tell You," "Mississippi Sawyer," and "Turkey in the Straw," sawed out on a squeaky fiddle by a popular player.

Picnic dinners were enjoyable. Each family brought well-filled baskets of meats, stewed and canned fruits, and pies and cakes. Bread was cooked in Dutch ovens. After a hearty evening meal and the end of the festivities, the picnickers could lie down on pallets and, looking up into the star-studded sky, fall asleep.

Some of the early settlers followed the tradition of an orderly, cultured life. Among them were found the leaders of church movements; for custom, education, and memory led them to observe the Sabbath and to promote Christian worship. In all but the smallest towns, some form of church services was established; and the pattern of this observance in one town was much like that of all others. Beaver City, with its brilliant, well-educated Rev. R. M. Overstreet, was outstanding for its Christian service.

Overstreet was one among those who had read the Beaver Townsite Company's highly colored advertisements of the proposed town in the valley of the Beaver; and in 1886 he had left Englewood, Kansas, in a light road wagon, bound for the land of promise. On his way south he saw little but horse and cattle ranches. At the divide between the Cimarron and the Beaver rivers, he saw the survey stakes and the first buildings of Neutral City, which consisted of a supply store, a saloon, and a blacksmith shop. Here he was entertained by two Baptist citizens and, because of their encouragement and help, preached to an attentive audience. Still farther south he came to the site of the proposed town of Nevada, but the streets and blocks were only wooden stakes marking future locations.

At a spring near the mouth of Camp Creek, he had his first rude awakening to No Man's Land poverty. An old, gray-headed man, with flowing beard, a hatless prairie Rip Van Winkle, was camped near the spring. His rickety "go-cart," a jaded horse grazing contentedly, a few traps beside the cart, and a half-dozen chickens headed by a game-looking old rooster minus a few tail-feathers all bespoke the grim, stark realism of poverty. But the old man was not downcast. "This is good enough for me," he told his sympathetic visitor. Overstreet drove on, feeling that there must be other similar homes in this dreary land, and that the region could have been more appropriately called "A Land Fit For No Man To Live In." Nevertheless, he reasoned, it was a land that needed his Christian ministry.

Finally, on a Sunday morning, he topped the sand hill above the valley of the Beaver and looked down at Beaver City. He crossed the stream and stopped his wagon near Lane's store, where he saw a group of cowboys lined up at the bar; a short distance back from the sandy street were loose horses grazing about a chuck wagon, as though a roundup were at hand. He was disappointed in Beaver, for here, too, misery, squalor, and hardship waited to crush the hopes of the people who would come to settle. But he was courageous and had the faith of the missionary, so he cast his gloom aside and rode back to Dodge City to bring his wife and children to their new home.

His belief in Beaver City's future was rewarded, for soon a bustling young town had arisen, with sod houses and shanties lining Douglas Avenue and cumbrous wagon trains, laden with all manner of things, plowing through the deep sand of the street. Overstreet preached his first sermon to a fairly large audience in an unfinished sod house on the avenue. Later, Rev. Robert Allen, a Methodist minister, came and worked harmoniously with him to meet the settlers' spiritual needs.

A few months after Overstreet's arrival, in 1887, enough Presbyterians had come to Beaver to organize a church and to plan a church building. Rev. Overstreet's Emporia friends contributed more than one hundred dollars for the structure, and the members in Beaver City helped with money and labor. Frank Laughrin freighted the lumber from Dodge City, others hauled rock for the foundation, and still others served as carpenters.

As the structure neared completion, its builders were eager to hold their first service in it. However, in their haste they had not protected the shingle roof from a stove-pipe; and during the first Sunday school session, the shingles caught fire from the hot pipe. Fortunately there was a ladder near by, and an active boy scampered up with a bucket of water and put out the fire.

This small church stood on the brow of a hill south of Main Street and overlooked the town. It was not large, but its tall spire could be seen from a distance, reaching high into the sky. Later, the Presbyterian church was to have a marked influence on Beaver's social life.

IX

Death of the "Road Trotters"

The bizarre, pulp-story type of outlaw escapades, killings, thievery, vigilance-committee justice, and border rawness of No Man's Land might well be doubted were they not adequately proved by faded letters, petitions, and other documents filed in the Department of Justice records of the National Archives. It should be remembered that lawlessness plagued No Man's Land more than neighboring regions, because it was without any kind of legal organization. At least in 1887 federal officials, from President Grover Cleveland down to the attorney general's field men, had many complaints about these lawless deeds.

Inevitably, deeds of outlawry increased in number with the influx of settlers. Marshal W. C. Jones of Topeka reported to Attorney General A. H. Garland on March 21 of this year that No Man's Land had become completely a rendezvous for outlaws, and that crimes were committed without fear of punishment. United States Attorney W. C. Perry admitted that conditions were bad, explaining that he was "almost daily in receipt of letters or information reporting crimes" there, but that the region was not within the Kansas District, or any other, and that there was no way in which the law could be enforced or crimes punished.

Were conditions in No Man's Land really as bad as Jones and Perry pictured them? Both stated that lawlessness was of long standing. There is every reason to believe that Jones and Perry did not exaggerate. Some proof is found in petitions from No Man's Land settlers, now found in the Department of Justice files. One of these petitions is headed by the name of J. M. Hill of Fairview, No Man's Land, and is followed by others. Hill wrote: "My boy was killed in June, 1886 at Neutral City; in September, 1886, William Williams was killed near Gate City; in November, 1886, Frank Van Deventer was killed near Neutral City; in February, 1887, a stranger was killed southwest of Neutral City; in July, 1887, Frank Kingston was killed at Fair View. Three men have been killed near Beaver City; three more have been shot and dangerously wounded, but recovered; numerous robberies have been committed; horse and cattle stealing is almost a daily occurrence."

It should be noticed that these crimes were committed during a period of only two years and that they occurred within the Beaver-Neutral City part of eastern No Man's Land. This distressful recital might have been duplicated in other parts of No Man's Land and in other years during which federal law did not extend over the country. But much the same kind of statements could have been made about the Kansas and Texas borders during the eighteen sixties and eighteen seventies. At best, Western border culture was raw and untamed, and passions were unrestrained.

In every No Man's Land community, settlers at-

97

tempted, although perhaps clumsily, to maintain law and order. Thomas J. Judy remembers that homesteaders in eastern No Man's Land were even opposed to the opening of saloons outside of the large towns. "In 1886," he said, "a party undertook to open a saloon in a tent located at the 'Tuttle' crossing of the Kiowa. By a gentleman's agreement amongst ourselves, we kept away from that tent and within a few weeks it had been moved away."

Only the petty thief and evildoer found his operations worth while in No Man's Land, for the settlers were poor. The professional gambler, such as was found in Kansas and Texas cow towns, found no lodgment in No Man's Land.

But claim jumpers were active, as in Kansas and Nebraska. The settler would no sooner start improvement on his claim than a heavily armed "road trotter," as a claim jumper was termed at Beaver, would appear to argue that the claim was his own. If the bona-fide settler protested, the road trotter would show him a stake he had previously driven down to establish prior right. As a rule, he had already located a large number of 160-acre tracts in this way, since he generally knew beforehand just where the immigrant intended to make his selection. If the road trotter had not already put a claim stake on that area, he would immediately do so. Invariably, he withdrew his claim if the homeseeker would pay him a small sum, usually about twenty dollars; and if the settler did not have the cash, the road trotter would accept a horse or other property.

Of course, the road trotter could not pre-empt all the choice land about Beaver, for there were many thousands of acres. Indeed, after a newcomer settled on a claim and built his cabin was the time when the road trotter usually appeared. Or if the settler and his family had left for town or a visit, the road trotter would occupy the house and maintain, upon the return of the family, that the claim had been abandoned.

Sometimes the road trotters banded together. At Beaver, Frank Thompson, F. E. Bennett, and the Tracy brothers, the dance-hall operators, formed such a gang. In fact, since Dick Roberts had sought to drive Widow Poggenberg from her claim, road trotting had grown to threatening proportions. Beaver City leaders discussed the growing menace as they met on the streets. Dr. O. G. Chase, Jim Lane, and J. C. Hodge were among those most active in arousing public opinion on the subject.

Chase had told his friends that if they could secure popular approval, they could set up their own government, since there was no federal control or agency. On October 26, 1886, a band of more than fifty men met in the Beaver sod schoolhouse to consider the formation of a government. After a lengthy debate they agreed upon six rules. First, they bound themselves to carry out and obey whatever rules they adopted; second, any person of legal age should be allowed 160 acres of land, if he had occupied it since April 1, 1886, provided he had broken five acres or made other equivalent improvement on it; third, any person could also hold a claim for each adult member of his family, including a father, mother, brother, sister, son, or daughter; fourth, each claimant must furnish a claim committee with written proof and description of his claim and of any other claim held for a member or members of his family; fifth, all those who had come in person to take, select, or purchase claims and had then gone away with an expressed intention to return should be entitled to the benefits and protection of these rules, and that all nonresidents who had claims surveyed and who had made no other improvements on them should have four months to settle upon them, otherwise their claims should be forfeited; and, sixth, that any person who should jump, trespass, or in any way damage the claim of a person complying with these rules would be told to get off such a claim, stop trespassing, and make good any damage done. If the committee's order was ignored, after the passing of twenty-four hours the committee would adopt "measures sufficiently severe to force compliance."

These rules were designed primarily to stop claim jumping, but rule three hit especially hard on George Scranage, an adventurer who had marked out a large number of 160-acre claims only by plowing a furrow around them. He had done this on the excuse that he was holding them for his relatives, but actually he had planned a neat swindle. The Portsmouth, Ohio, *Blade* had carried this advertisement:

Cheap Homes

McAllister & Scranage, locators of land in Neutral Strip, Indian Territory, can give you the best situation and figures on land. See Capt. A. J. McAllister on board the steamer Louise. Finest climate, best farms, purest water in the country. Titles clear and terms easy.

In far-off Washington, Congressman Payson's attention was called to the *Blade's* advertisement, and he

Courtesy Lawson Abstract Company

Looking east on Second Street, Beaver, in 1907. The first building on the left is Long and Munsell stable; the square white building, the courthouse. The Jones and Plummer Trail originally passed up the draw where the stable stands

Douglas Avenue, looking north from First Street, Beaver, about 1913. At the left is White House Hotel

Courtesy Lawson Abstract Company

promptly denounced it on the floor of the House. "Every man who publishes advertisements of that kind," he said, "or is in any way connected with them, is a thief and a robber. It is an attempt on their part to secure from the honest people of the country under false pretenses their money."

Scranage appeared little abashed by this public censure and went ahead promoting his land scheme, moving in and out of Beaver. Spears, the *Sun* reporter, said that while Scranage was away, the town marshal, Addison Mundell, seemed to act as his agent. Mundell told a visitor that if he wished to get in on the ground floor of choice Beaver property, he should write to Scranage in care of J. D. Ellison of Cincinnati, Ohio, who, it was reported, was furnishing Scranage with funds.

Beaver citizens seemed well pleased with their initial success in setting up a land-rules committee. They next circulated a petition signed by thirty-four men and one woman for a town meeting "to proceed at once and prepare a code of by-laws for our future adoption; also to prepare a form of quit-claim deed for our common use in the transfer of claims from one party to another." Dr. Chase presided over this momentous session, which, according to Spears, finally "resulted in one of the most unique Governments ever organized by civilized men." The minutes of it, as recorded in the "Record Book of Beaver, Neutral Strip," show that a "Respective Claim Board" was created to act as a temporary steering committee until a council could be provided by an election to be held on February 22, 1887.

Two actions of importance were adopted at this second meeting.

Sec. 3. To enable us to consolidate our strength, and to know the wants of the people of the whole territory, it is also suggested and hereby agreed upon that the entire population of Cimarron Territory turn out on February 22, 1887, and hold elections in their respective neighborhoods as near in conformity to law as possible, electing in each representative district three representatives, who shall meet in Beaver City on the 4th day of March, 1887, as a Territorial Council.

Sec. 4. To carry out the object set forth in the preceding section a President, Vice-President, Secretary, and Treasurer is hereby elected and authorized to act as a local council constituting a Board to be known as the Respective Claim Board.

Nothing in the minutes explains why the new territory was to be called Cimarron Territory. Certainly, it could more appropriately have been named Beaver Territory, for the Beaver River watered almost the entire length of the region, while the Cimarron merely cut across two of its corners. But Cimarron it was.

Section five required the Respective Claim Board to prepare a blank quit-claim deed form for the use of squatters. A claimant should file his claim with the secretary of the board, who in turn would issue a deed, unless a rival claimant objected. In this case, a committee of three would rule on the dispute. If, after its decision was made, either disputant was dissatisfied, a second committee of five would render a final decision. A fee of twenty-five cents was to be paid to the president and the secretary for each town lot deeded, unless it was to a non-resident, in which case the fee was five dollars.

The cattlemen of western No Man's Land did not share in the election of territorial delegates. Nevertheless, three delegates to represent them were chosen. The two meridian lines across the proposed territory cut it into three districts from which the nine delegates were to be selected. When Dr. J. A. Overstreet, secretary of the Respective Claim Board, received the election returns, he found the first council elected consisted of O. G. Chase, president; Merritt Magann, clerk; and R. M. Overstreet, J. G. Snode, Jim Lane, Robert A. Allen, Elmer Tompkins, Thomas Waters, and W. J. Kline, members.

Meanwhile, the Respective Claim Board had met its first severe test, which centered about road-trotter misdeeds. By Christmas, 1886, Bennett and the Tracys had abandoned their dance hall in favor of a dry goods and grocery business. They had much time to devote to road trotting, for their volume of business was small, and by forcibly evicting those claim-holders who would not meet demands for money and by firing into the sod houses of other settlers at night, they became a public nuisance.

Angry settlers reported the misdeeds to the Respective Claim Board; but before the Board acted, Thompson broke into Marshal Mundell's room and stole his Winchester. The town marshal had Thompson's sod house searched, rightly concluding that he was the thief. Thereupon Thompson in great anger threatened to shoot him on sight. His chance came a short time later when he met Mundell in front of the post office, and he would have killed him, had not Rube Chilcott grabbed his six-shooter and shoved it aside. Rube's prime concern was to protect by-standers, including women and children.

Still the Respective Claim Board hesitated to take action. Bennett and Charley Tracy took advantage of its timidity by adding insult to injury. A Kansan with two harnessed mules had stopped at the livery stable. The two road trotters watched him, wondering why the mules were harnessed and why the stranger was in a hurry to leave town. They concluded that he must have stolen the mules, and making themselves a self-appointed vigilance committee of two, they decided to take the mules from him.

They let the Kansan leave town. Then they mounted their horses and followed him to the home of a Kansas squatter, named Thomas Pemberton, where they found the mules in a corral. Pemberton evidently knew the two road trotters and suspected their intentions, for he greeted them coldly. The dialogue that followed is related by a contemporary and at least contains a modicum of fact.

"Is the owner of them mules here?" Bennett is reported to have asked.

"Yes," replied Pemberton.

"Well, we want him," Bennett said shortly.

"What for?" the squatter asked.

"Them mules was stolen and we want them and the thief," the road trotter replied.

During this purported conversation Pemberton was said to have been standing in his doorway. But when Bennett stated the purpose of his mission, he disappeared for a moment, then reappeared with a gun in his hand, saying, "You can't have the man or anything else you want!"

This was more than the road trotters had bargained for, so without pressing their claims further, they hastily rode back to town.

A short time later Charley Tracy joined Bennett to oust a settler named Hinton from his claim. When Hinton stoutly maintained his rights, they offered to let him keep two lots upon which he was building his sod house if he would pay them a small amount. But Hinton seized his rifle, said that he would not pay them anything, and they, too, withdrew empty-handed.

The gang's next and last misdeed was to pre-empt a claim which George Scranage was holding for his brother-in-law, W. J. Kline. To do this, Bennett furnished Thompson with lumber to complete a small dugout on the claim, which Thompson occupied to await developments. But Scranage was as stubborn as Hinton and refused to make a settlement. Instead, he and Kline appealed to the Respective Claim Board, which, driven to desperation, at last acted.

A large crowd attended the board's public hearing. Scranage and Kline vigorously denounced the road trotters and reviewed at length their past misdeeds. They argued that a crisis had come in the community's affairs and that the board must protect the rights and interests of all residents. The road trotters, in turn, attacked Scranage's illegal claim speculations, naming instances in which he had sought to swindle unwary land hunters. The attentive listeners who had crowded into the schoolhouse chiefly sympathized with Scranage and Kline, but it was noticeable that the Tracy and Bennett gang supported Thompson.

Thus the board was forced to choose the lesser of two evils, and after five hearings, on March 2, 1887, ruled against Thompson. Thompson angrily refused to obey the board's order to vacate, whereupon a posse quickly formed to oust him.

Scranage, Kline, and L. N. McIntosh (who was reported to have helped Scranage promote his land deals) had organized the posse by eleven o'clock, and the town seethed with excitement. Angry mutterings against the road trotters speeded the posse's organization. Its full personnel is yet unknown, although federal Department of Justice records supply the names of Billy Olive, a reckless man-about-town; J. C. Hodge, the postmaster; Lee Harlan; Addison Mundell; and Herbert T. Bright as other members.

At last the excited possemen, armed with rifles, shotguns, and revolvers, started from town toward Thompson's dugout in the side of a hill about two hundred yards west. Mundell brought up the rear, about one hundred yards behind the advance party.

According to Spears, Thompson watched the posse from his boardinghouse. Seeing Mundell trailing behind (as Mundell told Spears), he called out: "You — —, are you going to that claim? I'll stop you now." And he raised his Winchester to fire.

"I throwed my gun down," Spears reports Mundell as saying further, "and pulled as a man would shoot a bow and arrow."

But Spears heard a different story from two other eyewitnesses. They stated that when Mundell saw Thompson emerge from a stable door and start for his dugout, he leaped behind a sod wall to waylay him. And as the road trotter approached, Mundell opened fire. Only one shot took effect, and that struck Thompson in the right knee.

Thompson fell to the ground but managed to crawl to his house, and a woman who lived with him sent for Dr. Chase. Chase found Thompson's knee badly shattered and decided to amputate his leg. He therefore

bound it up as best he could and went in search of Dr. J.
A. Overstreet to help him with the surgery, leaving
Thompson on his bed in great agony.

Meanwhile, when the possemen heard Mundell firing, they ran back down the trail. Learning that Thompson had gone to his dugout, they then started in search
of his confederates. "They had started to run one man
out," wrote Spears; "they came back determined to kill
three men." In their quest, they went to Bennett and
Tracy's store to get two of them. Only Bennett was there,
for Charley Tracy had mounted his horse and fled to the
sand hills beyond the Beaver. Bennett was told that
Thompson, his friend, was badly wounded and wanted
to see him. Bennett probably suspected that all was not
right, but he was compelled to go nevertheless.

As the armed men entered the dugout with their
prisoner, Bennett saw Thompson lying on the bed. Bennett was smoking a big merschaum pipe and had just
raised his hand to take it from his mouth when he heard
the clicking of gun hammers. He whirled to face his
enemies and was met by a volley of shots. As he fell to the
floor dead, Thompson stopped groaning and begged for
mercy, but a shot rang out and he, too, was killed. Spears
identified his killer in this way: "Mundell justified his
killing of Thompson, even when helpless, on the plea that
Thompson had already tried to shoot him at the post
office."

Later, the posse returned to the Bennett-Tracy store
and told Pat Tracy, Charley's younger brother, that he
must close out the business and leave town. This he did
within two weeks.

Then, in keeping with the custom in orderly communities, a coroner and an inquest jury were chosen to render a verdict, which, after only a brief session, announced:

We the jury appointed to view the remains of O. P. Bennett and Frank Thompson, find that they came to their death from gunshot wounds received at the hands of many law-abiding citizens, thereby inflicting, as nearly as possible, the extreme penalty of the law as it should be in such cases. The deceased were bad citizens—one [Bennett] having run a house of prostitution and the other [Thompson] living in open adultery in our town. Each was accused of stealing and receiving stolen property, some of which was found on their premises after they were killed. They had each been firing into houses, holding a dozen or more claims, and driving honest settlers away from the country, and their untimely end is but the result of their own many wrongs. (Signed) J. A. Overstreet, M. D.; Laf Wells; James Deverie; Joseph Hunter; H. G. Wright; G. E. Myers, jurymen. O. G. Chase, Secretary.

At seven o'clock that evening the Respective Claim Board's meeting in the home of Dr. Chase had unusual interest for its members and for others who came. The minutes of the coroner's jury were read and approved, and then Chase appointed Rev. Overstreet to conduct the funeral of the road trotters. This was unusual, but not so much so as the board's action immediately after, when it created a committee of three "to consider the matter of issuing marriage licenses." Merritt Magann, H. S. Smith, and Laf Wells were appointed on the committee.

On the following day a cold, raw wind reddened the

sky with sand as a small group of stern-faced men followed a wagon bearing the bodies of the road trotters to
a site chosen for burial. There they listened to Rev. Overstreet read the dire warning found in the eighth and the
twenty-third verses of the Ninety-fourth Psalm:

Understand, ye brutish among the people; and ye fools,
when will ye be wise?

And He shall bring upon them their own iniquity, and
shall cut them off in their own wickedness; yea, the Lord
our God shall cut them off.

Then the bodies were dumped into shallow graves
and the crowd dispersed. After the funeral, Rev. Overstreet is reported to have said to Dr. Chase: "We will mold
public opinion and let the young men do the work."

The Respective Claim Board had named Overstreet,
Kline, and William Dow as administrators of the slain
men's estates, but there was little to administer. Thompson had left nothing. Bennett had some horses and an interest in the store, and these were sold to defray the cost
of the funeral.

X

Justice Without Law

For a time the killing of Bennett and Thompson stopped the "daring practice of heading off honest settlers," according to Rev. Overstreet. But in line with the principle of "blood toucheth blood," he believed that other deaths had to follow.

It will be recalled that Billy (W. P.) Olive was implicated in the Bennett and Thompson killings. In addition, he was undoubtedly guilty of some of the charges the coroner's jury had brought against the road trotters, for he was a known adulterer and cattle thief. A. M. McCoy, an early No Man's Land rancher, described Billy as "naturally wild, the son of a wild father" who had met a violent death in Kansas; and another reported that Olive had come from Smoky River, Nebraska, where "he had killed a man just to show that he was not afraid to kill one." At Beaver City, since the summer of 1886, he had lived "with slight labor," gambling and stealing cattle from near-by ranches, butchering them, and selling the meat in town.

The woman with whom Billy had been living decided to decamp while he was on a hunt in western No Man's Land. She charged that Billy, while drunk, abused her more than she could bear and said that this caused her to run away. But Billy returned from his hunt sooner than was expected, found her gone, and went in pursuit. He overtook her at Cimarron station on the Santa Fé Railroad. Fearful of the consequences, she told him that Bill Henderson, a Beaver City barkeeper, had caused her to leave by telling her that Billy had not gone hunting but had left her. Billy accepted the explanation and returned her to Beaver. There he confronted Henderson with the woman's story, which, of course, the barkeeper denied.

In spite of Henderson's denial, Billy still believed the woman. That night he and his henchman, "Lengthy" John Halford, spent many hours drinking and gambling, so that the next day he still nursed the supposed wrong and was ready for mischief. Still drunk, he and Lengthy re-entered the saloon early.

Henderson guessed that the two men were hunting trouble and watched them fearfully. Billy approached the bar, drew his revolver, and harshly ordered the barkeeper to set up the drinks or he would kill him. Henderson complied with the demand, for he knew that Billy was in a dangerous mood. Meanwhile, Billy shot the saloon lamps and glassware to pieces, and fired several shots into Henderson's trunk in one corner of the room. Then, after he and Lengthy had taken their drinks, they stalked out of the saloon.

A few minutes later Billy returned again, this time with a Winchester, and forced Henderson to walk in front of him out of the saloon and down the street.

From doorways and windows of business houses along Douglas Avenue, merchants, shoppers, and citizens watched the two men walking down the middle of the street. Billy maliciously struck and jabbed his frightened victim with the Winchester. Lengthy now joined Billy, and he, too, sought to impress the onlookers with his bravado by hitting Henderson with a revolver.

At last Billy raised his Winchester to fire into Henderson's back. But the cartridge failed to explode, whereupon Henderson started running, gaining speed at every jump, while bullets from Lengthy's revolver zipped past him, only accelerating his speed. Billy reloaded quickly and again raised his Winchester, took aim, and pulled the trigger; once more the gun misfired, and by this time the would-be victim had escaped.

Henderson hid in the sand hills beyond the Beaver, where a few hours later his friends found him. They urged him to return to town and "bushwhack" Olive, saying that the people were now aroused and eager to have Billy get his deserts.

He reluctantly accepted the suggestion and returned to Beaver City for his Winchester. Meanwhile, others carried Billy the news that Henderson was looking for him. Again Billy and Lengthy came on the street, searching in store after store. While they were crossing from the west to the east side of Douglas Avenue to look into the Garrigues store, Henderson, hiding behind a sod wall across Second Street, shot Billy through the heart and killed him.

The onlookers made no move to apprehend the murderer. Billy deserved death, they said. But they warned Lengthy to leave town, and that he did immediately, as fast as his horse would carry him.

This killing, which followed so closely that of Bennett and Thompson, caused Beaver City residents, more than ever before, to see the need of a town government. For this purpose, on September 15, 1887, an election was held. A druggist, Jake Thomas, was named mayor; Addison Mundell, marshal; W. B. Ogden, clerk; Dr. J. A. Overstreet, treasurer; and the commissioners were Jack Garvey—a saloonkeeper—and Thomas P. Braidwood, J. H. Alley, and Merritt Magann, merchants.

The new government was soon to have its first test. A short time after the death of Olive, two strangers from Beloit, Kansas, Eugene Brusher and John A. Clark (alias Andrew H. Morris), drove into Beaver City. After registering at the Blake Hotel, they went over to the Donnelly saloon for whiskey, and there met several idlers, among whom was Doc J. R. Linley. The local hangers-on lined up at the bar to drink with the visitors and to swap coarse jokes. Linley was thought to have come to Beaver the preceding summer with a young lady whom he had married with a license procured from a local official and thus of doubtful validity. It was also reported that he had left a wife and several children back in Iowa.

Doc Linley was a conspicuous figure in Beaver City; he wore a long Prince Albert coat and a silk, high-top hat, regalia that the cowboys tolerated because he was an amiable fellow. While he was drinking with the Kansans, Brusher turned to Linley and said, "Let me see how I will look with that thing on." Whereupon he took the hat and put it on his own head.

His companion, Clark, was quite drunk, but not too drunk to attempt to show his new friends that he could shoot the hat from Brusher's head. He drew his revolver and fired, but the bullet struck far too low and Brusher fell dead.

Clark "screwed up his face" and simulated grief.

Later, an investigator of the affair thought that for some time Clark had been looking for an opportunity to kill Brusher because of an old grievance. Clark tearfully protested that the killing of his best friend was accidental. Addison Mundell, the town marshal, had been playing cards in the back of the saloon. He hastened forward when he heard the shot, saw Brusher dead on the floor, and arrested Clark. He guarded his prisoner during the following night, since Beaver City had no jail.

Next day, Mayor Thomas arraigned Clark for a hearing, and the evidence in the case was presented to a jury, which, after deliberating for three days, brought in the surprising verdict of "guilty"—not guilty of murder, but of "criminal carelessness" in handling a lethal weapon! Clark was fined twenty-five dollars.

A few days later Brusher's brother, Bill, rode in on a Dodge City freight wagon. He examined the testimony in the case and then announced that his brother's death was an accident. After this he met and made friends with Clark, and for a few hours the two men were inseparable. That night when they were drinking together at Donnelly's bar, Brusher excused himself for a moment to step outside. But outside, through the saloon's only window, he shot Clark dead. Then he leaped on his waiting horse and fled. Mundell sent a fusillade of shots after him and a posse pursued, but the fugitive escaped.

Clark was buried beside Bennett and Thompson. His and Brusher's camping outfit was sold to pay the expenses of the funeral. Clark's death was another instance of border justice without law. The jury inquiring into Brusher's death had handled its case clumsily, but each juryman felt that the ends of justice were served.

Elsewhere in No Man's Land, lawlessness was just as threatening as at Beaver City. At Neutral City there was a saloonkeeper named Boone, a typical dead-beat, gambler, and ne'er-do-well, whose bar and gaming tables were frequented by many others of his kind. Bill Bridgford (alias McCoy), an Englewood, Kansas, gambler, was a chief habitué. Boone and Bridgford were said to have joined forces occasionally at cards to fleece local cowboys. It was for this purpose, on a June day in 1886, that Bridgford left Englewood for Neutral City. As he was nearing his destination, he noticed a woman and a child in a buggy, approaching from the rear. Instead of giving them the road, he turned with his revolver and fired two shots over their heads. The woman's two horses reared and whirled about, upsetting the buggy and throwing her and her child out; fortunately, she held on to the reins, righted the buggy, and drove rapidly in the direction from which she had come. Bridgford, doubtless enjoying the scare of the woman and child, rode on to Neutral City.

That night he and Boone arranged a game of poker with two unsuspecting cowboys, one of whom, named West, was from the Collar Ranch, and the other, Doc Douglas, from the YL Ranch. Just after the game had started, the Neutral City vigilantes came to the saloon for Bridgford. The *Clark County Chief* of June 21, 1886, tells what followed. "While they were a little time among themselves," the *Chief's* story ran, "some parties on the outside opened fire on the house, firing through the side on which there were no windows, thus placing the parties on the inside at a disadvantage. At the first fire a man known hereabouts as McCoy, but whose right name was Bill Bridgford, fell mortally wounded, the ball entering his right side and lodging in his abdomen, causing almost instant death. He lived long enough, however, to give the residence of his folks and how to dispose of his effects. Doc Douglas, who is well known in this section, was shot through the right arm, the ball crushing the bone in a terrible manner. It had not been fully decided as to whether his arm will have to be amputated or not. He is now in our City [Englewood] and doing well.

"Charlie Rockhold, the barkeeper, was shot through the thigh and a glancing shot on the head leaving pieces of the ball adhering to the head. His wounds are serious and may prove fatal. The man named Boone happened to be on the outside of the house opposite to the parties doing the shooting, looking after McCoy's horse. The assaulting parties opened fire on him, which he returned. Failing to get the horse's bridle, he rode off as he was at full speed, but before going far ran into a wire fence cutting himself fearfully. Turning, he started again, but before going far again collided with the fence, this time with such force that the throat of the horse was cut, killing it instantly. Boone then walked to a sod house and stayed all night. He was not wounded by the shooting; his cuts from the wire fence are very bad. The parties who did this wholesale shooting are yet unknown. . . . Doctor Holmes of our city dressed the wounds of the injured."

While the attack was in progress the vigilantes shouted, "Bring out Bridgford!" The shooting would not stop until he was run out—all inside could be killed. West answered that Bridgford was dead and that he, Douglas, and Rockhold were wounded and would come out. The firing ceased, and the wounded men filed out of the saloon with uplifted hands.

The vigilantes were only after Bridgford because of his brutal treatment of the settler's wife and child, but the cowboys and the barkeeper were told that they had been found in bad company and must therefore leave town. Douglas and West promptly did so, but Rockhold stayed on, saying that he was not responsible for Bridgford's sins.

Boone's saloon was burned to the ground by the vigilantes, and when Rockhold finally recovered from his wounds, he had to seek a new location. He built a sod house on a claim that had been pre-empted by the Bender family, and Bender vigorously opposed the pretensions of the blustering Rockhold. In a fight that followed, Rockhold shot and wounded Bender. That night the local vigilantes surrounded Rockhold's sod house and called on him to come out. Upon his refusal, one of their number, Frank Van Deventer, climbed up on the roof and poured kerosene on it. After he had performed his mission, he jumped to the ground in front of the only window, and Rockhold, watching from the window, saw him and killed him.

After the besiegers had set fire to the roof, Rockhold came out, fighting and running, and in the darkness of the night and the consequent confusion, he escaped with only two slight head wounds. He went to the home of a neighbor, who drove him to Englewood, where his wounds were treated. Later, he was given a preliminary hearing before a court at Ashland, but the presiding judge ruled that his court had no jurisdiction and that he could not force No Man's Land witnesses to appear.

Neutral City was connected with still another killing. Bill Williams, half-blood Indian, possessed the dubious title of Gate City's "bad man." Once he rode into Gate

City on a horse that was half-broken. He rode up to a store, dismounted, and made his horse secure by running his hitch rope through a crack in the door, fastening it from the inside with an axe handle. Later, when he was ready to leave, half-crazed with cheap liquor, he mounted the horse and dashed away without untying the hitch rope. It seemed that the whole front of the store exploded! The horse went end over end, as did Bill, who landed in a prickly-pear bed. Onlookers brought Bill into the store and placed him face downward on a counter. "We commenced pulling thorns with tweezers," says Fred C. Tracy, "pulling slowly, pretending a desire not to hurt him and for every thorn he let out a string of oaths."

A short time later, Bill rode over to Neutral City, which was then a town of two grocery stores, a general store, a drug store, a blacksmith shop, and a livery stable and a saloon—altogether one of the wildest towns in No Man's Land. He was accompanied by Fred Ailward, a harmless, good-natured cowboy. Late in the afternoon, after they had imbibed liberally of what the Neutral City saloon had to offer, and when they had made "the rounds of the town," they mounted their horses and started for Gate. On their way home they came to a sod house about one hundred yards back from the road, where a settler was chopping firewood while his wife sat on the woodpile watching him.

"Just watch how fast them settlers can run," Ailward later reported Bill as saying. Then he drew his revolver and fired over the heads of the settlers. With the sound of the shot, the woman jumped from the woodpile and ran for the house, her husband close upon her heels.

But this was not the end of the affair. The enraged

homesteader sortied out with a shotgun and dashed into his corn patch by a short cut to a point where the road turned the corner of his field. Here he waited for the approaching horsemen. Bill saw him crouching there and grabbed for his revolver, but he was too late. Buckshot from the farmer's gun almost tore his neck off, and Ailward was slightly wounded.

A short time later, the local vigilantes advised Ailward to leave, advice he promptly accepted, although he swore to the end that he was not responsible for Williams' escapades. He declared that, on the contrary, he had always advised Williams to refrain from violence.

XI

The Vigilantes in Action

Outlawry increased in eastern No Man's Land in proportion to the swelling inflow of homeseekers. Violence, thieving, and claim jumping forced the honest settlers to organize for their own protection. Blue Grass, Gate City, and Neutral City—all small sod towns—formed vigilance committees, each of action rather than of observing the niceties of judicial procedure. This suited better the settlers' needs.

Old Sod Town, an adjacent outlaw rendezvous, two miles north of the Texas line and one-half mile west of the mouth of Coon Creek, was as unsightly as its name implies. Standing irregularly and nakedly on the prairie were saloons and pool halls, one store, a blacksmith shop, a restaurant, and a shack that later served as a school. Rubble and refuse littered the space about the buildings, doors and windows were broken and unpainted, and building interiors were little more than dark, ill-smelling holes.

The town had no church building and even the school shack was used for only a four-month term. Here young Harry Parker came to learn his three "R's." "I do not recall the name of the first teacher I had in No Man's Land," he later wrote, "but I do remember that one or two of the older students carried six-shooters to school.

They would remove them and hang them on the wall by their hats."

Sod Town was a regular loafing place for cowboys, horse thieves, and bad men generally. The most notorious was the Chitwood gang of horse thieves who lived three miles northwest of town on Coon Creek.

But Lockwood, Sod Town's deadly rival, was equally tough. Two Kansans, Smith Ellis and Chance Fish, had started this town. It was three-quarters of a mile north of the Texas Panhandle line and one and one-half miles south of Sod Town. Sod Town's champion toughs were the Parson brothers, Al, Charley, and Lyman; while Lockwood had its Smith Ellis, Curley Mass, Bert Mc-Clure, and John and Sam Allen, according to Parker.

Parker remembers, too, a feud between these rival groups, growing out of a squatters'-right dispute to creek bottom land cornering on the southeast of the Parsons' claim. "The Parsons thought that they could bluff the others off the land. One day they opened fire with high-powered Winchesters at long range upon their opponents." Parker could hear the bullets whistling past him. The rivals exchanged several shots, never getting nearer to each other than a quarter of a mile. But this was too close for the Parsons. Lyman was wounded in the knee, and he and his brothers retreated.

"Al Parson's son, John, was my chum," said Parker. "I happened to be at the Parson's home when I heard some shooting, and John began to act nervous. I wondered what it was all about. Soon we saw the older Parson boys running toward the house carrying their Winchesters, and one of them was limping. Then I realized what had happened."

But "the Parsons still had revenge in their hearts." They operated a Sod Town store where "tough men" stayed, drinking and gambling. One night, when several of them were half-drunk, the Parsons "sent them to rob the Lockwood Store." Wash Stevens, head of the gang, was chosen to go into the store first. He walked in and demanded that Ellis give him his money. Ellis was standing behind the counter by the money drawer, which was near the door. He opened the drawer, pretending to get the money, but came up with a six-shooter. The two men exchanged hasty shots, the powder burning their faces but doing no other damage. Stevens fell out of the door flat on the ground to keep from being killed. This caused Ellis to believe that he had killed him.

Ellis then prepared to receive Stevens' confederates. He stationed himself in the back of his store, with the front door open just enough for him to see anyone approaching. And there he sat all night, with his Winchester across his knee.

One of Stevens' men did attempt to approach the door, and Ellis shot him. He lay there nearly all night calling for help. But no one dared to go to his aid, and he died. The next morning Ellis learned that he had killed only one man. After this affair, the Sod Town men kept their distance.

A gang of horse thieves, reportedly headed by Jim Chitwood, were among the worst offenders in this part of No Man's Land. Chitwood's main headquarters were on his Coon Creek "ranch," but he also maintained a way-station at Sod Town, from which stolen horses were driven to New Mexico, Texas, and elsewhere.

Settlers of Blue Grass, Gate City, and Neutral City

joined to break up this organized thieving. When the Chitwoods invaded, the three communities combined their vigilance committees to oppose them, with a strength of about two hundred men.

On one occasion the thieves had collected seventy-five horses at their Coon Creek hideout. They planned to drive them to New Mexico; and two boys, who came looking for work, were hired to make the drive. The youths started with the horses and had gone as far as the Pig Pen Ranch on the Palo Duro when the wrathful horse owners overtook them, made them prisoners, and brought them back to Cline, south of Gate City. Here lynching preparations were made. The lads pleaded that they thought their employers were honest ranchers who had put them in charge of a legitimate herd. The Cavius brothers, two former miners from Colorado, had known the boys previously and interceded for them. The youngsters were permitted to return home and admonished to stay away from No Man's Land.

When the vigilantes learned that the Chitwoods had a substation at Sod Town, they prepared to trap them there. A local mail carrier came to a vigilante whom he knew, and gave information which the settlers of Sod Town had been afraid to disclose. He said that while recently passing Sod Town he had noticed that all the Chitwoods rode fine horses and that the gang never seemed to work. The carrier had frequently seen herds of horses there, which upon his return would be gone.

The vigilantes carefully mapped their plans. They decided to attack Sod Town simultaneously from all sides, and thus give the outlaws no chance to escape.

The three vigilante bands were to meet a few miles

below Sod Town on an appointed night and from there each group would take its position before the attack, which was scheduled at dawn. When the time came, however, only the Blue Grass men were present. They waited for several hours and then decided to move alone against the outlaw town. The maneuver failed, for the thieves got word of their coming and fled in the opposite direction. When the vigilantes reached town, they captured only a cripple, Kit Chitwood, and his gray-headed father, who had taken no part in the thieving. Kit's feet had been frozen and amputated the previous winter.

Later, the Gate City and Neutral City vigilantes arrived, too late to be of service. From a distant hill members of the Chitwood gang watched them. The vigilantes did not attempt to run them down, for they knew that the thieves were riding fast horses and could outdistance them as most of the attackers were mounted on plow horses. Aware that there was little chance of capturing other members of the band, the vigilantes rode back to Neutral City with the two prisoners. There they put them in a sod livery stable and stationed both day and night guards over them.

The dramatic events which followed are somewhat clouded in controversy. Three years after the capture of the Chitwoods a federal examiner wrote a brief for the attorney general which detailed conditions in eastern No Man's Land. The report stated that in April, 1888, Sheriff Shughrue of Clark County, Kansas, had been handed a warrant to arrest one George Montgomery for horse stealing, and that the sheriff in turn had sent his deputy, George Gillen, to No Man's Land to make the arrest. Clark County records show that Gillen was not a deputy;

early residents identified him as a member of the vigilance committee sent after the alleged horse thief. The federal brief stated that Montgomery had stolen "horses" in No Man's Land, but a surviving member of the vigilance committee said it was "two mules and one horse," which was probably right.

The vigilantes overtook Montgomery as he was on his way back to Kansas and captured him. He pleaded with them to surrender him to the Clark County sheriff; but, after they had forced him to admit his thefts, according to a contemporary authority, they took him to Neutral City and put him in the livery stable prison with the other two prisoners.

On the night of April 15, a band of Blue Grass vigilantes came to the livery stable and demanded that the guard surrender Montgomery to them, saying that they were going to hang him. According to a Gate City vigilante's version of the affair, the guardsmen demurred, stating that they had no authority to surrender him, that others felt it would be better to take him to Sheriff Shughrue and claim a $300 reward to use to finance an expedition against horse thieves then often rendezvousing in the Cheyenne Indian country. But the Blue Grass men announced that they were there to hang Montgomery, whatever might be the opinions of others, and the guard made no effort to stop them.

The contemporary account states that forthwith Montgomery was seized and brought to the center of the sod room. There, under a protruding, overhanging roofpole, he was forced to mount a box; one end of a rope was put about his neck; and the other thrown over the roof pole. Seeing that his captors were about to hang him, the condemned man begged them again to surrender him to the Clark County authorities. But they would not listen. They told him that he must hang and that if he had any last request, he should make it.

He did have a last request—that young Chitwood be brought before him. Then followed a dramatic scene. The terror-stricken cowboy stood on a box with a rope about his neck, and denounced Kit for being responsible for his thieving. When he had named the personnel of the thieving band, he finished speaking. Kit later said that Gillen did the hanging; but local tradition has it that the vigilante leader (named as Roger McCoen in an affidavit) asked that every member of his band put his hands on the rope so that all would be equally responsible for the hanging, and that this was done. The box was then kicked from under the condemned man.

The vigilantes also would have hanged young Chitwood, but one of the guards ridiculed the executors. "If you couldn't take the real thieves," he scoffed, "why should you hang a defenseless cripple?"

A Kansas farmer had joined the vigilante raid on Sod Town so that he could recover two mules which the Chitwoods purportedly had stolen. He now approached his new friends and asked that they agree to exchange Kit for the mules. The vigilantes accepted the suggestion and sent word to Kit's uncle that they were willing to talk terms on this basis. Otherwise, they would hang his nephew.

The federal examiner's brief tells that J. K. Casteel of Florence, Colorado, drove to Neutral City in a wagon belonging to the elder Chitwood. He came to secure the release of the two prisoners. Casteel later stated that the leader of the vigilantes told him that the two men would be hanged shortly unless Casteel paid the captors $800 worth of property—presumably the new wagon, new harness, and a fine span of mules—and that he took some time to consider the offer before he finally rejected it. The vigilantes then took the mules anyway. This story is doubtful, since Casteel's affidavit was questioned as much as Kit's.

The vigilantes said that Kit's uncle came with a good span of mules, new harness, and a new wagon to make the exchange, but not the Kansan's mules. The Kansan hesitated to accept the exchange, saying that he only wanted the return of his own mules, since they were pets. But when he was told that this could not be, that his mules had already been driven out of the country and sold, he finally accepted the exchange and drove back home.

Later, states Harry Parker, the vigilantes returned to Sod Town and found Jim Chitwood eating dinner at the Johnson restaurant. When he saw who the visitors were, he leaped to his feet, seized the Johnson girl, who was attending the table, and using her as a shield, backed out of the rear door and escaped.

Boss Neff of Hooker, Oklahoma, furnishes an interesting postlude to this Chitwood narrative. In his diary he relates that some time later Wash Stevens was at the Neff ranch on the Palo Duro and while there confessed to Neff and his brother Ira that he was a former member of the Chitwood gang. He stated that he was now on his way to New Mexico or Arizona to settle down and "to follow a path of rectitude." About 1886 [8], he said, he and the Chitwoods were in southeastern No Man's Land stealing horses, that a vigilance committee came looking for them, but that they escaped and later established themselves in the rugged country of northwestern No Man's Land.

Of course there was less violent, but just as effective, vigilante action. A typical instance was a trial held near the Tuttle Trail crossing of the Kiowa, in eastern No Man's Land. Settlers organized a kangaroo court to protect themselves, selecting Judge Lambert, J. T. Stewart, and T. J. Judy as judge, sheriff, and attorney. Stewart brought some horse thieves before Judge Lambert, Postmaster Spencer was appointed to serve as counsel for the accused men, and the trial started. Judy, the kangaroo attorney, won his case, and the thieves were given ten days to quit the country. In passing sentence on the culprits, the dignified and impressive sixty-five-year old judge gave them a lecture, saying that no neighborhood of good men, women, and children could tolerate lawlessness, and furthermore that he wanted to disabuse their minds of any thought that the sentence was harsh. He would give them ten days to leave the country, but within these ten days their rights and interests within the community would be protected by all the residents. Any delay on their part after this time, however, would be a mistake. The thieves probably saw the point, for they left long before the ten days had expired.

When it became known throughout No Man's Land and adjacent country that the vigilantes were on the march, cattle and horse thieves fled before them. By 1890 there was a marked decrease in offenses of this kind. And it is a significant fact, too, that these sod towns—Gate City, Neutral City, Lockwood, and Sod Town—spawned in poverty and crime, soon passed into the oblivion of ghost towns.

XII

The Wild Horse Lake Tragedy

No Man's Land vigilance committees had handled surprisingly well its outlaw problem by 1888, but they could hardly be expected to prevent rival Kansas factions from riding into the region to stage a massacre. And this is just what happened in July, 1888. This bloody affair grew out of an intense rivalry between two Kansas towns, Hugoton and Woodsdale, dating back to a county-seat struggle of two years' standing.

In the beginning, the county-seat struggle had centered about two forceful leaders, C. E. Cook and S. N. Wood. Cook had resigned as postmaster at McPherson in June, 1886, to accept the management of the Hugoton Town Company and proved to be a resourceful leader in promoting the interests of his town. But he met his equal in Samuel Newill Wood. Wood was born at Mount Gilead, Ohio, on December 30, 1825, and came to Kansas twenty-nine years later. At first, he settled on a claim near Lawrence and became the leader of the free-state party. In later years, he served four times in the Kansas legislature and one in the senate. In addition, he established the first newspaper at Cottonwood Falls, at Council Grove, and two newspapers at Woodsdale, a southwestern Kansas border town that bore his name.

In the Stephens County–seat war, Wood's legal maneuvering against Hugoton had been so successful that residents of that town in desperation had kidnapped him and had held him for a short time in No Man's Land, all to no purpose. This seemed only to accentuate his fight on Hugoton. Then he persuaded Vorhees voters to join with Woodsdale in floating county bonds to induce a railroad to build through the county, passing through Vorhees and Woodsdale but leaving Hugoton off of its route. Of course, Hugoton residents bitterly opposed this move; and at a council meeting called to consider the matter, Sam Robinson, Hugoton's city marshal, became involved in a quarrel with a Woodsdale champion and discharged his pistol. A short time later, Ed Short, a Woodsdale constable, went to Hugoton to arrest Robinson; but in a fight there, Short and two companions were driven out of town.

Both Short and Robinson were men of questionable reputations, according to one authority. So Short's treatment at Hugoton brought bad blood between these two men. A few days later, on Saturday, July 21, 1888, Short learned that Robinson, Charles and Orin Cook, and A. M. Donald, with their families, had gone fishing in No Man's Land. Now, Short seemed to think, was the opportunity to arrest Robinson without interference; therefore, with two other men he left Woodsdale bound for the fishermen's camp. When they had come within one-half mile of it, Short sent a note to Robinson demanding his surrender. The Cooks advised Robinson not to give up but to mount his horse and escape, for if he remained and refused to surrender and a fight ensued, he would endanger the lives of the women and children.

Robinson accepted this advice and fled from camp in the opposite direction from the Short party, which immediately gave chase. The pursuers finally cornered Robinson but were unable to take him; consequently, Short sent a messenger to Woodsdale to ask Sheriff Cross to raise a posse to come to his assistance. It should be stated here that already Robinson held a grudge against Cross for having beaten him in the county election for sheriff. For this reason, Cross knew that Robinson would not surrender; therefore, he deputized Robert Hubbard, C. W. Eaton, a youth named Toney, and one other to go with him, and on Tuesday evening they started southward. But when they came to the place from which the messenger had started for Woodsdale, they found neither Robinson nor Short.

Meanwhile, the fishing party hastened back to Hugoton, carrying the news of the raid of Short's posse; and the thoroughly aroused townsmen presently had organized an armed band of men to go to Robinson's rescue. They overtook Short's party and a running fight followed, which ended about dark, on July 25, the Woodsdale party escaping.

On the same evening, Cross's posse started back to Stephens County, having failed to overtake Short or to find Robinson. For hours they had ridden fast, and now their horses were fagged. About nine o'clock they came to a haymakers' camp at Wild Horse Lake, some walking and some riding. This camp was about eight miles south of the Stephens County line, in present-day Texas County, Oklahoma. Here Cross and his men stopped to rest and to rebuild the strength of their jaded horses. Cross and two others of his party staked their horses near the hay camp, and lay down to rest at the foot of some hay-stacks. The other two men climbed into a near-by wagon. All of the men left their Winchesters and revolvers a short distance away with their saddles.

Back in Hugoton at four o'clock that same afternoon, a second posse had been organized to go to the assistance of Robinson. This party consisted of twelve men, six in buggies and six riding horses. After several hours' travel, they stopped for supper, when, much to their relief, Robinson came to their campfire, having escaped Short and his men. A rider was promptly sent to Hugoton to inform Mrs. Robinson that her husband was safe, and those remaining moved on toward Wild Horse Lake to camp for the night.

Robinson and the six horsemen of the party took the lead and the others—C. E. Cook, Orin Cook, Cyrus Freese, Jack Lawrence, J. B. Chamberlain, and John Jackson—followed in the buggies.

The advance party reached the hay camp about 10 or 10:30 o'clock that night. It was a bright moonlight night, the moon shedding its rays over the prairie with the brightness almost of day. There before him, Robinson saw Cross and his men sleeping and quickly deployed his men to surround them before they could awaken.

Then, while those coming up in the buggies were yet several hundred yards away, they heard a shot from a Winchester break the night stillness; so they hastened forward.

Cross was awakened by Robinson's shout for him and his men to surrender. "We have you surrounded on all sides and you cannot escape," Robinson stated.

Since Cross and his men were several yards from their

The Massacre at Wild Horse Lake, Neutral Strip   A. A. Forbes

The massacre at Wild Horse Lake, from a photograph by
A. A. Forbes

The first hour's work on the Beaver Railroad

t Hours Work on the BEAVER R.R.

weapons, there was nothing to do but comply with Robinson's demand. This proved to be a mistake. Quickly Robinson's men stepped forward to search their prisoners for arms but found none. Then Robinson, standing several yards away, said: "Sheriff Cross, you are my man," and raised his Winchester and shot him down. Just as indifferently, he next turned to Hubbard, who stood transfixed, and added, "I want you, too," and killed him also.

Chamberlain had just taken young Toney's revolver when Robinson's second shot rang out. So he, too, took aim at his victim and fired. Toney dropped to the ground with a flesh wound in his shoulder, for he had turned his body slightly to avoid receiving the bullet. Now seeing that his life was in deadly peril, he feigned death. Robinson and others of his band shot the last two of Cross's men as they climbed out of the wagon. All this massacre required but a few moments of time. Then, before leaving the camp, to make sure that all the men on the ground were dead, one of the executioners approached and fired a second shot into each body. When he came to Toney, Chamberlain told him that a second shot was unnecessary, for he had taken careful aim. It was only this stroke of luck that saved the youth's life.

Robinson did not harm the haymakers, but told them to follow him back to Kansas. Then he and his party rode away, leaving four dead men and one wounded on the ground.

Toney's wound was bleeding profusely, and each moment he was becoming weaker. His position was desperate, for unless he could have medical aid soon, he would also die. Although he staggered from weakness, he managed to mount his horse and ride away from the camp littered with its dead. About noon the next day, he rode into Vorhees. The news of the massacre had preceded him, and already a party of men had gone out to bring in the slain men's bodies. A local officer wanted to take the wounded lad to Liberal, Kansas, where he could have medical attention and would be safe from Robinson and his men, when they learned that he had not been killed. But he was too weak to stand the trip and was hidden in a cornfield until a Woodsdale party arrived and took him away.

The Wild Horse Lake tragedy was a signal for residents of Hugoton and Woodsdale to rush to arms. The two towns were like military camps, with guards stationed at strategic points, with travel restricted, and with both armed forces put in a state of tense expectancy.

Throughout all these events culminating with the killing of Cross and his men, Wood was Hugoton's indefatigable enemy; and after the massacre, he was no less active. Fortunately, three companies of state militia restored order in the two towns; but Wood was not content to let matters rest. In November, he succeeded in having the United States district attorney arrest a score of Hugoton men, on the grounds that a conspiracy to murder had been formed in Kansas, thus giving the Kansas court jurisdiction. Judge Foster, however, refused to support his attorney's action, ruling that his court had no jurisdiction over acts committed in No Man's Land.

Wood, like an avenging nemesis, next turned to the Texas courts, first to the Northern District of this state, where the judge refused to act. "It has been over a year since these cold-blooded murders were committed in No Man's Land," Wood wrote Attorney General Miller, on

May 5, 1889. "And the law of last winter in cases of felony gave the Court of Paris, Texas, jurisdiction. . . . Is it possible that these cold-blooded murders are to go unpunished?"

This seemed to give him a cue, for he next appealed to Judge Bryant of the newly created court at Paris for the Eastern District of Texas. Promptly, Judge Bryant ruled that his court had been given jurisdiction by act of Congress, as mentioned in Wood's letter to Miller, and he directed his grand jury to investigate the case. As a result, twelve Hugoton men were arrested and held for trial.

The men thus held appealed to Judge Brewer of the United States Circuit Court for a discharge on a writ of habeas corpus, on the grounds that no court had jurisdiction over No Man's Land; but their petition was denied, and they were held for trial in the July term of court.

This tardy court action came too late, however, to punish the chief offenders. Robinson had fled to Colorado, where he was shortly arrested for robbing the mail and was sent to the penitentiary to serve a sentence of twenty-two years. The other horseback riders who first came to the haymakers' camp the night of the massacre had also escaped. One had fled to Belgium, a nation that had no extradition treaty with the United States; and nothing further was ever heard of the other four.

Meanwhile, the trial of the twelve Hugoton men started, with young Toney as the star witness for the prosecution. The testimony in the case, now on file in the National Archives, runs into hundreds of pages. The magazine *Green Bag* carried an article on the trial, stating that Wood was in Hugoton between the indictment

and the trial trying to arouse prejudice against the accused men. Then, with the opening of the trial, he went
to Paris with his witnesses. "In the preparation and trial
of the case, he was the real prosecutor, the district attorney having been a mere figurehead. Wood had freedom
to subpoena whomsoever he saw fit, his list of witnesses
running something like three hundred, many of whom
had no knowledge of the matter or men. A coach-load of
this class of witnesses reached Paris at six o'clock one
evening, registered the following morning, were then
excused by the prosecuting attorney, received their certificates of attendance, averaging perhaps a hundred dollars each, and started home the same day." This author
stated that Wood bought such certificates, where he could,
which, with his pay for services as deputy marshal, netted
him a handsome sum, variously estimated at from $10,000
to $15,000.

Six of the twelve men put on trial proved an alibi;
and six—C. E. Cook, Orin Cook, Cyrus Freese, Jack
Lawrence, J. B. Chamberlain, and John Jackson—were
found guilty of murder and sentenced to be hanged on
December 19, 1890.

In sentencing the six men, Judge Bryant asked each
one if he had anything to say. C. E. Cook accepted this as
an opportunity to make a speech in defense of himself
and his friends, a stirring recital that was read over the
nation and aroused general sympathy for the condemned
men. Four of them had served in the Union Army. C. E.
Cook was a member of the Kansas Traveling Men's Association, and all were members of the Knights of Pythias
or the Knights of Honor. Cook appealed to these organi-
zations for contributions to aid him and his friends in

their defense, and generous gifts were made. As far away as Nashua, New Hampshire, the boyhood home of the Cooks, $2,200 was raised for the case; and Judge Freese of Ohio, brother of one of the condemned men, also brought a large sum, the whole of the donations reaching about $5,000.

Because of these contributions and a writ of error, the case was taken to the Supreme Court, with George H. Peck and W. H. Rossington, assisted by J. F. Dillon and Judge Freese, as the condemned men's attorneys, each of whom volunteered his service without cost. Attorney General Miller, who appeared for the federal government, acknowledged the error and remanded the case to the Paris court for a rehearing.

Then Miller also sent Judge Horton to Paris, as his special agent, to make a full investigation of the killing and of the trial; and upon his subsequent report, the district attorney who prosecuted the case was dismissed for his faulty work, which had cost the federal government more than $100,000. Judge Bryant was also reprimanded and barely escaped dismissal.

Now arose an extraordinary problem—the case was still pending, although a petition for its dismissal signed by thirty-eight of the forty members of the Kansas Senate and by all the state officers had been sent to President Benjamin Harrison. Since Kansas was a Republican state, naturally Harrison, a Republican president, gave the matter due consideration. He properly referred a decision in the case to the Attorney General, and that worthy likewise passed the matter on to his first assistant, who refused to render a decision.

But it seemed that at last fate moved to solve the

problem. Wood was killed by a man named Brennan, and Short likewise fell before an enemy's gun. Wood's partner committed suicide, and three others of lesser note who were interested in the prosecution either died naturally or met violent deaths. Thus, those who pushed the prosecution were presently either dead or had lost interest; so at the fall term of court, in 1895, the case was stricken from the docket.

Throughout the period from the time of the killing of Sheriff Cross and his men until the Paris trial, No Man's Land appeared in the news reports over the nation. That Congress had made a blunder in not attaching this region to some state or territory seemed clear to all, but that it should still delay the establishment of courts there was inexcusable. Everywhere people joined with No Man's Land settlers to demand that corrective measures be taken.

No people were more interested in the proceedings of the Paris court than those of Beaver City. Since 1886 they had fought an uphill battle to protect their homes and town. Now they witnessed the rise of an indignant public opinion against the dilatory actions of Congress. Timing their move to gain the support of neighboring people after the Cross murder case had been remanded to the Paris court, V. Metzger, Tom Braidwood, James Lane, and R. M. Overstreet presented Attorney General Miller with a petition, on February 3, 1890, again asking for legal protection.

The petitioners recited that during the many months since their town was established "they had to contend with well organized bands of outlaws," and that no United States court afforded them protection. "Under such trying circumstances, men who were never accustomed to resort to extreme measures before or since, were forced to use them or be sacrificed." They were especially incensed that the Attorney General's Office would permit a situation wherein their townsmen were dragged "700 miles away from our business and from the community, witness the facts, and so become victims of Texas U. S. Marshals and others who may connive with them for the gratification of gain and personal spite."

But truly, there was a silver lining to the black cloud over No Man's Land. Law and order, long delayed, was about to come, bringing peace and security for men and their property.

XIII

Paper Wads *vs.* Leaden Bullets

The steps taken towards the emergence of the "Territory of Cimarron" amidst chaos and lawlessness are unique in American constitutional history. The first step was a "Call for a Mass Meeting to be held at Beaver City, November 29, 1886," the manuscript of which, signed by thirty-four men and one woman, is yet kept by Beaver citizens.

In answer to the call, more than one hundred residents crowded into the sod schoolhouse to hear Dr. Chase explain why the meeting was necessary. Chase was well educated, a physician from New York, who prior to his coming to Beaver had promoted a real-estate division at Pueblo, and now had hopes of engaging in similar activities in Beaver. He was a man of extraordinary adaptability, energy, and resourcefulness, and was unusually well qualified to assume the chair of this mass meeting, to which he was elected. Another physician, Dr. J. A. Overstreet, was elected secretary; and J. C. Hodge, the town postmaster, was named treasurer.

Then in typical American fashion those assembled drew up "Rules and Regulations" to guide them in this initial move. The first was to define the bounds of No Man's Land; the second, to create three representative districts by the 101 and 102 meridian lines; and the third, to call for an election on February 22 of the next year to select three delegates from each district to form a territorial council, which should meet in Beaver City on March 4, following.

As provided by the mass meeting, the election was held on February 22, 1887, but voting was largely confined to eastern No Man's Land, and principally Beaver City. Therefore, at noon on March 4, those chosen as delegates assembled at the school house to begin their deliberations. When Dr. Chase, acting as temporary chairman, rapped for order, Dr. Overstreet, secretary of the Respective Claim Board, arose and read the names of the delegates elected. They were Chase, Alf. W. Burnett, Rev. R. M. Overstreet, Rev. Robert A. Allen, J. G. Snode, James Lane, Elmer Tompkins, Thomas Waters, and W. J. Kline. In their preliminary organization, the delegates named Chase as president, Dr. Overstreet as secretary, and Merritt Magann as clerk.

Burnett and Waters did not appear to answer to their names at roll call, leaving only seven men to transact business, but they were men who were "fairly up to the Jefferson standard—capable, honest, sincere." They were nondescript in appearance, bearded, some dressed in jeans, hickory shirts, and coats worn slick by much wear; but at least four of the seven were college men and all knew the basic principles of constitution- and law-making. Few Western territorial councils had delegates better fitted for their work.

When the council was ready for business, Rev. Overstreet slowly rose in his place to address the chair. He said that he had found a grave defect in the Constitution of the United States which he hoped would not be repeated in any similar document which they should adopt for Cimarron Territory. Then unfolding a manuscript which he held in his hand, he read and, after reading, moved the adoption of this resolution:

Whereas. The residents of Cimarron Territory are without the protection of law of any state or recognized territorial government, and recognizing the urgent need thereof, and desiring to adopt and establish rules and laws for our protection, safety, and government, do hereby recognize Almighty God to be the Supreme Ruler of the Universe, the creator, preserver, and governor of individuals, communities, states and nations, and recognize the laws of the United States as our organic law, and adopt the same with the Constitution of the United States as the foundation, and basis of all laws or rules for our government, and in so far as may be to execute the same.

Therefore, be it resolved by the representatives of Cimarron Territory in Territorial Council assembled that we do hereby declare ourselves the Territorial Council of Cimarron Territory, and do hereby adopt the Constitution of the United States and the laws thereof, as the ground work and foundation for all our laws and rules to be adopted for our government.

This resolution was unanimously approved. Two others were also adopted. The first divided the Territory of Cimarron into seven representative districts or counties—Benton, Beaver, Shade, Springer, Turner, Kilgore, and Sunset respectively—of four rows of townships, each taken vertically across the territory. The second called for an election for the first Tuesday after the first Monday in November, "for the purpose of electing nine senators and fourteen Delegates, who shall meet on the first Monday in December, A. D. 1887, as Territorial Council."

This, said a member of the council, ended their work on the Constitution of Cimarron Territory. Next, they turned to the making of laws, one of the first of which was proposed by Delegate Tompkins, so anomalous in its provisions as to be worth quoting here.

Be it resolved by the Territorial Council of Cimarron Territory in Council assembled that regularly ordained ministers of the Gospel are hereby authorized and empowered to solemnize the rites of matrimony for parties having first procured from the Secretary of any Auxiliary Council, a certificate authorizing such ceremony between the parties therein named, which certificate shall, with the return of the officiating minister endorsed thereon, be returned to the Secretary having issued the same within thirty days from the performance of such ceremony.

A fee of $1 shall be charged by the Secretary issuing such certificate, and he shall keep a true record of all certificates issued and returns to him of marriages solemnized, and local Secretaries shall make semi-annual returns thereof to the Territorial Secretary. Such certificates shall only be issued by the Secretary to parties that he is satisfied are of legal age and able to make a civil contract.

Delegate Snode's resolution was then adopted providing for the appointment of a committee of five to provide for the framework of territorial organization and elections. The right of franchise was given "to every male person lawfully domiciled in or an inhabitant of said territory at the time of said first election, being twenty-one years of age and a citizen of the United States or who had declared his intentions of becoming such."

Following Snode's resolution, two motions were approved. Tompkins again took the floor to move the calling of a general election in December to name nine senators and fourteen delegates to succeed the present councilmen, a proposal that was unanimously adopted. Then Delegate Kline asked for a judiciary committee to draft rules, laws, and regulations for the control of "communities, towns and the rights of claimants to land occupied, improved, held or claimed by residents of the Territory," which was also approved.

At the second council meeting on April 5, only five delegates were present, so President Chase appointed C. B. Beason as temporary clerk to take the place of Magann, who with Kline had resigned, feeling that there was little chance for Congressional approval. Then Chase read his executive message. He said that "this territory will never become a part of the states of Kansas, Texas, Colorado, or New Mexico, but on the contrary you gentlemen composing this Council constitute a legislative body" as distinct from other states as any territory. He urged that they enact laws that would elicit the envy of good citizens and the hatred of evildoers, for in so doing they would speak for a mass of nearly 10,000 people, with a rapidly increasing immigration. "They are our constituents," he added, "although many of them may not realize that we have a law-making power among us."

It was quite true that a large portion of the settlers living beyond the trade territory of Beaver did not realize that they had such a government. Rev. Overstreet later stated that they ignored the council's legislative enactments. He said that the council could only shoot paper wads; leaden bullets made a more lasting impression on defiant outlaws. Therefore, the statutes enacted were never enforced or observed any more than if they had been drafted for the inhabitants of the moon, and the sympathies of the settlers in central and western No Man's Land were just about as far removed.

The interest of the territorial delegates waned rapidly after the first two meetings. The "Journal of Proceedings" shows that at the July 5 assembly, Thomas Waters had failed to qualify and George H. Healy of Alpine was named to succeed him, and that C. B. Beason had resigned and President Chase had appointed W. B. Ogden, his son-in-law, to take his place, acts which the council approved later. In spite of this waning interest, the council stayed in session long enough to provide for three territorial newspapers as its official organs, to publish its proceedings regularly. Immediately editors Elmer E. Brown and George Payne succeeded in having their Beaver *Territorial Advocate* named as one of these. Also before adjourning, the delegates authorized their president to fill any council vacancy; but even this procedure fell short, for the council was forced to adjourn on September 6, October 4, and November 1, because of a lack of a quorum.

Settlers outside the Beaver trade territory were not only uninterested in the council's proceedings; they felt piqued at Beaver's attempts to govern them. In June, 1887, John Dale of Alpine wrote to Senator Cockrell of Missouri asking him to suggest some way in which No Man's Land people could prevail on Congress to provide for their welfare. Cockrell replied that they should elect a delegate to go to Washington to confer with Congress. Dale accepted this suggestion as good advice and relayed it, including a call for a nominating convention, to every part of the Strip. The response was enthusiastic. In July, 1887, convention delegates came from every precinct to the little town of Rothwell, eight miles from Beaver.

They came "on horseback and in every kind of vehicle, singly and in groups, all at their own expense, no two dressed alike, or looked alike, representatives of as many classes, callings and occupations in former days as individuals, different in tastes, habits of life and education; mostly strangers to each other but all intent on doing something, and interested in what might be done; thus from every direction the motley wayfarers rolled into this new political mecca. Being westerners, they soon became acquainted with each other, their interests were common and they were citizens of a common country. The atmosphere was redolent with patriotic sentiment. They were a throng of American citizens without a country, in search of their lost country and exultant at the prospect of finding it again. They settled down at their respective quarters. Every house in the village was packed with the visiting statesmen. The commons were quietly seized, horses staked out and private camps pitched in the woody groves for the convenience of the overflow."

The temporary chairman, A. B. Hulet, rapped the convention to order and read the roll call. The delegates were enrolled; and then Snode, of Beaver, a member of the territorial council, was elected chairman, and E. E. Eldridge, former editor of the *Advocate,* secretary. Rev. Overstreet was also an influential delegate and had high hopes of going to Washington, since Dr. Chase had promised to support him. But Chase, a shrewd politician, wanted to go himself, and did nothing to advance Overstreet's candidacy. Indeed, he influenced the slumbering territory's executive committee to ignore the actions of the Rothwell convention and to call a Beaver election which named him as the official delegate. He was able to swing this coup because of the influence on the committee of his rotund son-in-law, Ogden. Thus he had the backing of the council, the official seal of which was affixed to his commission.

But the Rothwell convention, after considerable jockeying, named John Dale as its delegate; and he more truly represented No Man's Land, since he was selected by delegates from every part of the region. This was the only time that delegates forming a genuinely representative body had sat together. Nevertheless, the chances of success of either delegate were seriously impaired because of this division. To puzzled congressmen, both men presented credentials; one, the endorsement of No Man's Land's Council; the other, a commission from the Rothwell convention.

No Man's Land now had its political factions. Two upright, self-willed, stubborn leaders, Chase and Overstreet, were so opposed to each other as to make compromise impossible, thereby destroying the "peace of Abraham." Chase posed as the self-appointed, ambitious, and impetuous promoter; Overstreet, a righteous, sturdy Scotch Presbyterian, indignant because Chase had tricked him.

In November it was the Beaver community again that elected the delegates and senators to the new council, for no one of them lived over thirty miles from town—another reason why settlers elsewhere had little interest in the council. In all, nine members of the new legislature met on December 5. Secretary Ogden called the council to order, and on motion of "Senator" Braidwood, "Senator" Joseph Hunter was elected chairman pro tempore, and J. E. Bundy, secretary. To guarantee at least a second session, Council Bill No. 10 provided for a general election in each precinct, town, or neighborhood throughout the territory on the first Tuesday after the first Monday in November of each year, for territorial, county, and precinct officers.

Since there were only nine senators and delegates present, they sat in joint session. Whenever it was essential for either the senators or the delegates to act separately, that group not so obligated would adjourn; but this was seldom necessary. Moreover, they presently remedied their attendance problem by empowering their presiding officer to drop the names of willful absentees and appoint others in their places.

The council provided adequate measures for repairing the roads and building new ones, but as there was no way of collecting taxes to pay for road officers, no overseers were elected. Beaver moved ahead with its own road program. The *Territorial Advocate* sent out a call for volunteers to work the streets, and almost the entire man power of the town turned out and put the streets and the Jones and Plummer Trail in fine condition.

No doubt, the most useless enactment of the territorial council provided regulations for railroads and corporations. It was reported that the council president was at one time connected with C. P. Huntington, the railroad builder, and had hopes of having him build a railroad through No Man's Land. Probably the most sensible enactment was one adopting the statutes of Colorado for the region, although they were never given wide use.

Rev. Overstreet later wrote that Chase dominated the new council, even after he had gone to Washington. Chase had instructed the council before he left for Washington, and "repeated the same by letter, to continue in session, keep up appearances, do something; make the biggest show possible." And, he added, some of the delegates were "abundant in resources and had plenty of wind," among them C. W. Bugby, a late arrival from Kansas, and Doc Linley. "Tom Braidwood was the comedian of the outfit," Overstreet said, "and Chase's right hand man. Tom was for all the fun there was in it, and he was just the one to keep alive and perpetuate the show." He would move consideration of "his favorite bill No.— asking an appropriation from the general government to establish at Beaver a storage battery into which electricity might be conducted from the clouds and conserved for use as a motor power for all kinds of machinery. . . . This scheme was especially demanded for No Man's Land, as electric storms and wind were her principle commodities."

The No Man's Land factional split was carried to Washington. There Overstreet had powerful friends, one of whom was Senator Preston B. Plumb; while Chase, upon his arrival in Washington, made friends with the radical element in Congress, including Greenbacker James B. Weaver. Springer of Illinois and Burns of Missouri also supported him, since they were proposing that all the lands west of the Five Civilized Tribes be opened to settlement.

December 12, 1887, was an eventful day for Dr. Chase, a quiet, bewhiskered little man, whose brow was deeply etched with wrinkles of worry, as he sat in the House gallery to listen to Representative William Springer of Illinois present to an attentive session of Congress his petition on behalf of No Man's Land settlers. The House had given this aggressive Illinoisan permission to read it. Springer introduced his subject by saying that there were "at least 10,000 American citizens . . . in the said territory; that they are without the protection of local or general laws; that they have been compelled by the necessities of their situation to establish, and they have established and are maintaining, a provisional government, by and for the people, in form truly republican, for their common protection, safety, and welfare."

Continuing, he said that justification for the setting up of a government over this part of the public domain of the United States rested upon the settlers' necessity to organize for self-protection and defense, an inalienable right of local self-government.

For the most part, Chase's petition was an excellent No Man's Land historical summary, from the arrival of its first settlers until the present, stating why a claim board and a territorial council had been set up. In conclusion, he asked for the right to sit in Congress, so that he could properly inform its members on matters pertaining to No Man's Land or its problems.

Springer then asked "that the petition and certificate of Owen G. Chase, claiming to be elected a delegate from the Territory of Cimarron, be referred to the committee on the Territories, when appointed; and that pending the consideration of the organization of a Territorial government, Mr. Chase be entitled to the privileges of the floor of the House, the same as is now accorded to contesting members."

When he had sat down, and after Representatives Mills and Dunham had asked questions about Chase's petition, the floor was yielded to Representative Peters of Kansas.

Peters strongly supported Springer's resolution, stating: "There is now no law to protect them in the property they may take with them into the territory; there is no law that protects them or their property from violence while in the territory; there is no law in that section by which they can collect any obligation that may be contracted with a settler upon this No Man's Land. There is the utmost need of some legislation touching this land, for it is virtually outside of the pale of the law, and outside the United States in that respect, although geographically within its limits." He favored extending to Dr. Chase, "an old gentleman of most excellent character," the rights then accorded contesting delegates.

But it was not to be. Others present felt that it would be unwise to depart from regular procedures in such cases and demanded that Chase's request to sit in Congress be also referred to the committee on territories, and Springer finally yielded.

Of course, Dr. Chase was greatly disappointed in not being extended the honor of sitting in Congress. But he had achieved a major success: congressmen had listened to his presentation of the needs and problems of No Man's Land, all of which those who engaged in the debate following the reading of his petition acknowledged. So he returned to Beaver with the assurance of House and

Senate leaders that Congress would soon act in behalf of No Man's Land.

Dale had also been given an attentive hearing by members of Congress, but he had not received the recognition granted Chase. According to Rev. Overstreet, he had secured the location of new post offices and regional fish spawns.

The Cimarron Territorial Council continued in session, enacting a number of laws which proved useless because of its lack of funds and thus power to enforce them. It made an attempt to tax the ranchers, but angry cattlemen challenged, "Go ahead and try to collect it." In fact, throughout its existence, the council lacked power. "It was not stillborn; it was abortion," said Editor Brown. Nevertheless, it had discouraged outlawry by using "paper wads" instead of "leaden bullets."

Chase again went to Washington during the winter of 1888–89, in the hope of being seated in Congress and drawing his salary; but he failed in both objectives. Then he served as a lobbyist for the opening of "Old Oklahoma" to permanent settlement.

XIV

Ebb and Flow

As the green of spring crept up the valley of the Beaver in 1887, the first immigrant wagons from Kansas arrived in Beaver City, now a bustling village of 600 to 1,000 residents. Editors Brown and Payne took note of the newcomers in the *Territorial Advocate,* forecasting a settler flood-tide by midsummer, when they said there would be "hundreds arriving each month."

Beaver townsmen prepared to receive their share of this immigration. With spades and shovels they dug away Douglas Avenue's large sand dunes and brought in clay to form a new street surface for pounding hooves and wagon wheels. Some of the merchants had prospered so well that they tore down their sod shanties, built pretentious frame structures, and made plans of hope and optimism.

Still, the town's pressing problem was that while it was the capital of a No Man's Land, no great improvement could be made until Congress came to the settlers' rescue, granting them a land office and making provisions for the completion of land surveys, for courts, and for schools. At every council meeting, the delegates and senators petitioned the President and Congress on these subjects. They felt that they deserved as much attention as Old Oklahoma, a region not half so large as No Man's Land. Their "territory" had a population of 15,000 settlers, villages and towns, schools and churches—all won under the handicap of squatters' rights.

Federal postal records prove their claims. They show that five post offices were established in No Man's Land in 1886: three along the eastern boundary, Gate, Benton, and Blue Grass; Optima, northeast of present Guymon; and Carizzo in the northwest corner. In the next year, there were ten: six east of Beaver and three west, but all nine in present Beaver County. And in 1888, there were ten others: six in Beaver County, three in Texas County, and one in Cimarron County. Only two, Murdock and Peoria, were established in 1889.

Along with these post offices, dozens of small villages had appeared, many of which were ill advised and doomed to become ghost towns with the passing of years. J. H. Abbott has listed fifty villages of this kind, although he does not mention Beer City, an infamous community just inside the boundary of No Man's Land opposite Liberal, Kansas. J. R. Spears described it in 1889 as being "composed exclusively of disreputable houses, the only village of the sort ever heard of in America." Most of the No Man's Land villages, however, were law-abiding, typically Western communities, usually made up of a general store and post office combined, a blacksmith shop, one or two other businesses, and a half-dozen or more residences.

At first the older settlers of No Man's Land cordially greeted the new arrivals from Kansas, Nebraska or Iowa and sought to advise them. They warned them against

depending on farming alone for a living, for crops were
uncertain and markets poor. They also advised that they
stick to the valleys of the streams, for there they would
find good land and water. One squatter said, "160 acres
ain't enough to support a man"; and another stated,
"This is a poor man's country." If the new settlers expected more, they had better leave now while their teams
were strong enough to pull their wagons out. No doubt,
these more experienced homesteaders had been depressed
by adversity, or they secretly desired to keep the new
settlers out of the country so that they could have "elbow
room."

Much to the chagrin of the old settlers, the later arrivals did much as they pleased. They took small 160-
acre claims and put their sole dependence in farming,
settling the prairies away from the streams, as they were
advised not to do. As for its being a poor man's country,
a recent arrival told a group of Beaver farmers that their
country was poor only if they made it so, implying, of
course, that industry and thrift could make a change.

The old settlers resented this attitude, and the rift
thus created widened with the passing of months until it
finally caused the rise of political factions. In 1888 some
of the newcomers backed a council ticket headed by
"Doc" Linley for president and a Gate moonshiner, one
"Captain Hubbard," as a delegate to Congress. Hubbard campaigned actively, said an old settler, delivering
lengthy orations and moonshine whiskey; and this coali-
tion ticket won. Secretary Bugby stamped and sealed the
commission of Hubbard, who hurried away to Washington to curry the favors of such congressmen as Senator
Ingalls of Kansas. "And when Congress passed the organic

act establishing the Territory of Oklahoma, including No Man's Land," wrote Overstreet, "the curtain rung down, and Hubbard remained the last of the Mohicans."

There were also "would-be" cowboys among the late arrivals, according to another settler. They amused no end the experienced cowmen when they "appeared on the streets with high-heeled boots; spurs with bells; big saddles with mohair-covered pockets; leather or mohair chaps; broad-brimmed hats, often with rattlesnake bands; rawhide ropes; red bandannas; fancy quirts; and Navajo blankets. It was amusing to the few older cowboys still here to see them strutting around, trying to walk bow-legged, so it would appear that they were born in the saddle. Hi Koller said he was going to hang an old boot on the side of his bridle and see if the damned fools would imitate him."

Much of the old settlers' advice was sound. During the summers of 1886 and 1887, the No Man's Land farmers made fair crops, even on the prairie land away from the streams, but there was little demand for what they raised. When they hauled their cane and maize to Kansas towns, they received a mere pittance. Even No. 2 wheat sold in Dodge City for only forty to fifty cents per bushel.

No doubt the newcomers had cause to remember the old settlers' remark that No Man's Land was a poor man's country, for 1888 was a lean year. Hot winds, blowing day after day from the southwest, blasted and withered June crops, and a prolonged drought finished their destruction. As a rule those homesteaders who had planted their first crop had expected to pay after the harvest what they owed the local merchants; but with no crop to do this, they faced hard times such as they had never known.

Food was scarce throughout No Man's Land. Bread, flour gravy, and molasses were the common fare. If occasionally the settler could add wild plums which he had gathered along a near-by creek, or a jackrabbit, or other game, this was a luxury. The federal government shipped in beans, salt pork, and other foods, which some of the drought-stricken people accepted. But the old settlers scoffed, saying that they had never asked the government for anything except protection and titles to their lands.

Then came exciting and hopeful news. On March 23, 1889, President Harrison announced that on April 22 following, at high noon, Old Oklahoma would be thrown open for settlement under the Homestead Law. Here were more than 1,800,000 acres of land, as fine as could be found in the West, and free to those who could register their claims first.

Long before the opening date, wagon trains, one after the other, moved southward over all the roads crossing No Man's Land, pointing toward this new land of promise. Many hundred settlers joined this "Oklahoma parade."

Yet a large number of the first settlers stayed on. "Don't worry," one remarked, "they'll be back!" He had become acclimated and had passed through other trying periods and did not propose to leave now.

But he was mistaken. Most of those who moved out— more than 6,000 settlers—never returned, except to cross No Man's Land on their way to Kansas or elsewhere. E. A. Enfield wrote a few years past that his family returned to Kansas. He said that "most every settler had abandoned No Man's Land and their homes and that region was in possession of the cattlemen again." His father hitched two cows to his wagon. "The load for the cows was such a drag," he said, "that father and mother and the older children walked most of the way on the return journey. En route back to Kansas we met people leaving No Man's Land in much the same circumstances."

No doubt some of those Enfield met were perennial movers. The lure of greener fields enticed them. They wanted to see what was around the next bend of the road, or over the hill. And, of course, most of them did not secure claims in Oklahoma and probably would not have stayed had they been successful. For many years later, their rickety, travel-stained covered wagons, burdened with their household effects, pig crates, and chicken coops, with plows and stovepipes tied to coupling poles and pulled by gaunt oxen, horses, or mules, could be seen on every well-traveled road. They were the late nineteenth century nomads, progenitors of modern unemployables.

Those who stayed on their claims in No Man's Land became the basis of a hardy and self-reliant folk—a plains people, made up of settlers from twenty-two states and six nations. Among the newcomers who remained was the former Union soldier, who drew a pension from the federal government. "This was his invested capital," said Rev. Overstreet, "with his own teams that he had brought, his household and farming utensils, an extra horse or two, perhaps a cow or so, and a few pigs; and, in some cases, the prolific hen. He could build a sod house, fairly comfortable with his own hands, absolutely without expense. He could gather up buffalo and cow chips for fuel off the prairie. . . . In this way he could make a start on a very small capital and easily rustle a sort of a living."

Factionalism would not down. Presently a rump faction headed by Linley, Hubbard, and Bugby, and supported by other disgruntled elements, held the reins. Sessions were largely given over to the reading or discussion of petitions for Congressional action on their claims. And these, when added to previous efforts, at last brought victory. Already measures had been introduced in Congress to give No Man's Land the relief it wanted. Senator Plumb had offered a bill to attach the region to Kansas for judicial purposes; Representative James Burns of Missouri had introduced another during the winter of 1887–88 to create the Territory of Cimarron; and a third would make it a part of New Mexico. But all these failed. At last, on May 2, 1890, Congress approved the Oklahoma territorial bill attaching No Man's Land. At least in name, No Man's Land ceased to be. Under the organic act, it was merely labeled Oklahoma's seventh county, with its county seat at Beaver City; but when the territorial legislature met at Guthrie, the temporary capital, it became Beaver County.

However, it was largely in name only that No Man's Land ceased to be, for a long hard struggle yet awaited its settlers before they could claim their land and rise to an economic status equal to that of a neighboring area. Another year passed before the earlier land surveys were completed and squatter claims could be registered properly. The homesteaders' rights were recognized, and they were allowed to count three years' residence, if they had lived in No Man's Land that long, toward the total five-year period required before final ownership.

Bonfires were lighted by the jubilant settlers everywhere, from the east to the west, when news of the passage of the organic act reached them. At last they had won everything for which they had asked—civil government, a land office (in Beaver), provisions for schools, and courts.

There were cowmen, however, who questioned the new order, especially Judge Buford's court at Beaver City. In later years Judge Cotteral told an interesting story of how a near-revolt by the cowboys was quelled.

When Judge Buford arrived in Beaver City, he brought with him Deputy Marshal Chris Madsen, for he feared that there might be trouble. He was compelled to hold his court session in a room over a saloon, of which there were several in town. An alarmed citizen brought him the news that there were "roughnecks" in the saloon below organizing to break up his court. Promptly he sent Madsen downstairs to see what could be done.

When Madsen entered the saloon, he saw the three ringleaders lined up at the bar, taking a round of drinks, talking loudly, and making threats. Madsen went into action; and when he got through, one of the toughs was shot through the hand, a second was struck over the head with a six-shooter, and the third was handcuffed.

Madsen marched the three thoroughly cowed trouble makers up the stairs and before the astonished Judge, saying, "Judge, the rebellion is over!" The men were put in jail and given an opportunity to think about the vagaries of the law.

Next, Madsen was told that the manager of the nearby ranch where the three imprisoned cowboys worked was on his way to town to kill him. When the rancher rode up, Madsen was standing in front of the saloon awaiting him.

"What do you want?" he asked the surprised cowman.

"I came to kill that deputy marshal," was the reply.

"All right, I'm the man," Madsen said, "and I want to tell you just one thing. You climb back on your saddle at once and leave town, or there will surely be a killing. Get back quickly and gallop as you leave."

The rancher took another look and recognized Madsen, who had the reputation of being the best pistol shot in the Southwest. So without another word, he remounted and galloped away.

While hundreds of No Man's Land emigrants awaited the soldiers' signal guns to start "Harrison's hoss race," as the Oklahoma opening was called, their neighbors back home were experimenting with wheat raising. An early resident says that in this year for the first time wheat was raised as a money crop.

Still another change was made in 1889. When the several thousand settlers moved out of No Man's Land to find new homes in Old Oklahoma, cattlemen, who had overstocked and overgrazed the adjacent range lands, came in. Since their cattle were too poor to drive to market, they sold them to No Man's Land farmers on long-time credit, as low as nine dollars a head for cows with calves. In later years farmers who had made these purchases became owners of small herds, thus laying the basis for a new farm-ranch industry.

For the next ten years, Beaver County's population had its ebb and flow. The Rock Island Railroad built from Liberal, Kansas, diagonally across the region, causing such towns as Tyrone, Hooker, Guymon, Goodwell, and Texhoma to spring up and settlers to occupy the uplands of what is now Texas County.

Since Beaver County had displaced No Man's Land,

those other towns that had survived the exodus to Oklahoma breathed a new spirit. Among these was Hardesty, at the junction of the Coldwater and the Beaver, a short distance from Beaver City. It had a newspaper, the *Times,* that was an enthusiastic booster for Beaver County part of the time and Hardesty all of the time. On July 19, 1890, it reported that a thrifty class of people were settling in the county, and that the "time had passed when a man's life would be in danger should he go up a draw and bawl like a calf."

But the *Times* was presently dethroned as Hardesty's chief booster by the *Herald* under Dick Quinn's editorship. Quinn never tired of directing his shafts at rival towns, toward those editors who made disparaging remarks about Beaver County, and in preaching the gospel of good lands, excellent water, and abundant resources. To him, Hardesty was in the center of Beaver County's best lands; and it had the additional advantages of being at the crossroads of important trails and on the survey of the Rock Island Railroad, that had already reached Liberal, Kansas.

Yet in spite of editorial ballyhooing, there was little increase in the population of Beaver County.

For several years writers occasionally referred to Beaver County as No Man's Land, much to the annoyance of its settlers. In March, 1893, the editor of the Wichita *Eagle* made this mistake. Immediately he was challenged by Editor J. C. Hodge of the *Advocate.* " 'No Man's Land.' What dense monumental, assinine ignorance!" he thrust. "Call us 'McGinty' if you choose, but in the name of your protection from an idiot's asylum, don't call us 'No Man's Land.' " When the Kansas City *Star* carelessly used the term "desert" in referring to Beaver County, it met with a similar reproof. "The editor must have been intoxicated or chuck full of pure cussedness," Hodge retorted. He pointed out that Beaver County had shipped more cattle to Kansas City than any other ten counties of Oklahoma, and any ten counties in either Kansas or Missouri.

But Quinn was more versatile, his editorials at times sparkling with humor. On April 5, he observed that "March went out like a lion and April was ushered in in the same manner. . . . Frank Davis and Howard Maxwell arrived last Sunday with a house which they moved from Zonsville, Grant County, Kansas, a distance of about 85 miles. . . . On the next trip they will bring down a deep Kansas well which they will convert into ready made post holes for use in fencing their claims." And on August 16 he noticed that "The Joyous cowboy of yore is fast fading away—he's no more. He used to be gay, naturally restless and very emphatic when he was bowling up. He wore $7 pants for everyday, used silver mounted bridle bits, a pearl handled six-shooter, but was satisfied with beans, bacon and black coffee at the chuck wagon. Now he wears blue over-alls, wants sugar in his coffee, demands oatmeal for breakfast and smokes cigarettes. And where he used to set in dollar stacks, he is now contented with an ante of 'one come-along two.' "

Just when it seemed that editorial boosting would bring immigrants to Beaver County, two events nullified the efforts. The first was the opening of the Cherokee Outlet for settlement, in September, 1893. Editor Hodge never ceased to warn his readers against a Beaver County stampede. As early as March 16 he wrote that strangers were in Beaver seeking one of Uncle Sam's free farms and that they did not care "whether the Cherokee Outlet was ever open for settlement or not." In August, he boasted that "very few if any in this section contemplate taking in the Strip boom, whether through curiosity or any other reason," although he may have been whistling in the dark.

As the time approached for the opening of the Outlet, the movement of covered wagons across the Kansas border became heavier each day. The La Crosse (Kansas) *Chieftain* made mention of this, stating that a prairie schooner had just passed through town bearing on its cover this inscription: "In God we trusted, and in Colorado busted. Let her rip; we're going to the Cherokee Strip." But the *Chieftain* counseled against hasty action.

The *Beaver County Democrat* ridiculed reports that the Outlet was the answer to the "farmer's dream." "We don't claim that Beaver County is a land of milk and honey," he wrote, "where you will find roasted turkeys on tree branches ready to be taken and eaten by the hungry and that manna is showered at our doors, but we do claim that you can get a good homestead here for as near nothing as any place on earth." Editor Quinn of the Hardesty *Herald* supported this point of view, writing that it was folly to purchase land in the western part of the Outlet for $1.50 per acre when the same quality of land could be found in Beaver County almost free of cost.

It is hard to estimate how much restraint these newspaper writings had on Beaver County settlers. It is certain that several hundred left, but it is equally true that the general exodus of 1889 was not repeated.

The second event was the reappearance of drought and hot winds. An Arkansas City report to the Beaver *Democrat* of September 15, 1893, compared the wind to "a blast from a furnace." The morning had opened bright and clear, but as the sun approached its zenith the air began to heat up and the wind to blow from the west, hot and searing, turning "the fields of green crops from green to black in a day." The local United States Weather Bureau report of three days later read: "We are now passing through one of the longest sieges of drouth ever experienced, no rain has fallen for twenty-two days and the present prospect for rain is not encouraging. A severe hot wind prevails over nearly all of the two territories."

Again the Panhandle settlers felt hard times and again some loaded their wagons and left their claims and the country. But Governor William C. Renfrow's annual report to Secretary of the Interior Hoke Smith showed that the Beaver County population of February 1, 1894, was still 2,316. Yet, this was the second time within four years that the population of the region was sifted; and, according to Governor Renfrow, those who were left composed a "thrifty, industrious, and enterprising" folk. Although experiencing incredible hardship, they had taken "possession of the virgin soil with nothing to depend on save their grit and energy and labor, and [had] builded homes, opened successful farms, and planted orchards that are today the wonder of the world."

The town of Beaver suffered more than neighboring villages during 1893. For by a presidential order its land office was merged with that of Woodward, a new Cherokee Outlet village.

Beaver citizens had other handicaps also, their most pressing problem being their common schools. Here their shortcomings were many—poor school buildings, little or no equipment, untrained teachers, any kind of textbooks the pupils brought to school, and almost no funds to make improvements. During their emergency, however, business and professional men and women who could instruct in the "three R's" volunteered to teach; and where the school term was only four or five months, they prolonged it by charging a small fee, usually one dollar per month. Mrs. Mary England stated that at the end of a subscription school she taught near Tyrone, she received "one pig, six chickens, some beef from one family and a quarter from another,"—and two dollars in cash!

Each year Beaver City sponsored a normal institute to encourage and train these volunteer citizen teachers. The *Beaver County Democrat* of July 14, 1893, carried an enthusiastic account of such a session. Those who attended were given the advantages of refresher courses. Professor R. E. Dickson taught civil government and physical geography to a "flourishing" class; Miss May Overstreet offered instruction in grammar, history, theory and practice, didactics, composition, and also led the exercises in calisthenics. No wonder she was "always appreciated" by the teacher who was fortunate enough to know her. Superintendent Errett, one of Beaver City's physicians, instructed in physiology and arithmetic, "to the entire satisfaction of all." Brown said that the good doctor never seemed to be in deep water, for "as to physiology he is always at home, and he can apply names to some muscle or other that we wonder at not dying with the horrible lot of stuff in our makeups." Miss Ollie Crawmer had charge of political geography and reading, but during the session of the institute she left for El Reno, Oklahoma, to secure a certificate to teach there during the fall.

There is little doubt that these institutes promoted teacher training and greater interest in schools. In November following, the versatile Dr. Errett, now serving as the county superintendent, reported that out of Beaver County's forty-three school districts, twenty-three were "in running order."

In time, before 1907, when statehood was granted to Oklahoma, conditions changed materially. Sod schoolhouses were supplanted by frame buildings, teacher training was improved, and more funds were available to pay the teachers, to buy equipment, and to lengthen the term to six months or more.

Perhaps the saving grace of the Beaver County people throughout the trials of the territorial period was their desire to keep up their social activities. Dances, picnics, play parties, and spelling bees were as popular as during the time when there were few settlers.

A typical instance of their whole-hearted enjoyment of a picnic was the much-heralded July the Fourth celebration at Beaver City in 1893. For weeks prior to this date, Editor Hodge of the *Advocate* had written approvingly of the proposed event, as did also Editor Joe H. Carter of the *Beaver County Democrat*. On June 25 the latter printed the full program which included songs by the glee club, a welcome address by Joseph Hunter, an oration, and dancing and fireworks in the evening.

As a result of this publicity, men, women, and children came, in every conceivable conveyance, on horseback, in buggies, hacks, wagons, and on foot, some arriving by sun-up. The whole town of Beaver was enveloped in dust, and its streets were thronged with a jostling, good-natured crowd, all bent on fun and frolic, shouting, laughing, shaking hands, and renewing old acquaintances. The hotel, the wagon yard, and houses with rooms for rent could not accommodate those who came; so they camped on vacant lots and in the cottonwood grove on the south bank of the Beaver River. They were there from every part of eastern Beaver County and some from as far away as the Black Mesa country, old and young, big and little, homely and handsome. Flags and bunting fluttered from doorways and windows, and the irrepressible "Young America" celebrated noisily with firecrackers.

Among those who came were "gray-headed and serious looking patriarchs," who mingled with colorfully attired lasses, "staid and somber appearing matrons," the sturdy yeomanry that "politicians delight to bamboozle about election time"; and occasionally there was the "crowing and kicking baby who for the first time sniffed the air of a Fourth of July." All, the old and the young, thoroughly enjoyed the morning program—Hunter's welcome address, the selections rendered by the glee club, and Professor Walden's sensational and new "Talking Machine," announced in advance as "Edison's Improved Phonograph, the marvel of the age."

The noon hour was up to expectation. Most of the families had brought well-filled dinner baskets. But for fear that there would be some who were not prepared, the townsmen had made adequate provisions for all. One sumptuous dinner was spread at J. Thomas's for about forty persons, superintended by three local women—Mesdames Cartmel, Bogue, and Cummins; and another, equally appetizing, was spread in the Chase Opera House by Messrs. Hunter and McCool, where the guests were served lemonade, fried chicken, herring, bread and butter, beef, cakes, cookies, and other delicacies.

The afternoon was equally enjoyable. The older people listened to Miss Ollie Crawmer read "The Liberty Bell" and to Talcott Ormsbee's rousing oration on "Liberty," its history from the time that King John signed the English baron's Magna Charta until it was won in the New World on American Revolution battlefields. If the program seemed "a mite too long," the generous listeners conceded that July the Fourth came only once a year. There were a few, however, who wandered over to Chase's Opera House to listen again to the phonograph, or who watched the impromptu horse races, where ambitious youths were given the opportunity to prove the mettle of their nags.

The day was full of good things, but those who came were not yet satisfied and carried their revels far past midnight. In the evening all enjoyed the firecrackers, Roman candles, and skyrockets, watching enthralled their variety of colors and figures. After this, in Linley Hall, the string band struck up its toe-tingling melodies, and the boys and girls tripped through their accustomed waltzes, quadrilles, and polkas. Indeed, it was not until the next morning that the last of the revelers left for their prairie homes.

Sowing the Wind

Persistently the stigma of "No Man's Land" clung to Beaver County in spite of its citizens' protests and editorial reproofs. The region's monotonous, wind-swept prairies, its isolation, and its droughts, hot winds, and blizzards all combined to keep alive its traditional name.

Experienced homesteaders found that the region was not so poor as it seemed, that if they pursued several different labors, they could provide for their families. Many of the crops raised in the areas from which they came could not be grown on these high plains, but imported drought-resisting red kaffir, maize, African millet, broomcorn, Jerusalem corn, and cane could be grown profitably. When crops were poor or the market offered low prices, the homesteader learned to seek employment in the distant Kansas wheat fields, on a ranch, or in picking up buffalo and cow bones to sell. Leaving his wife to care for his family, sometimes he would be away from his sod house several weeks during the year engaged in one or more of these pursuits.

Many homesteaders would not submit to such a frugal and rigid discipline and moved to more inviting fields after months, and sometimes a year or two, of trying experience. This caused an ebb and flow of the population. Thus more than 6,000 settlers, in April, 1889, joined the movers bound for Oklahoma; and four years of hard times caused another exodus, but not so great. For the third time, during the period 1897–99, the exodus was repeated. The Territorial assessor's returns of 1897 showed the population of the county to be 4,778, but during the next two years it again declined, to 2,548. In Beaver County the homesteader had five years before he was required to "prove up" on his claim and an additional two years before he must pay taxes, or a total of seven tax-exempt years. No doubt some settlers moved out as the deadline neared to escape paying taxes.

The assessor's estimates revealed that Beaver County had 3,681,000 acres of land, only 426,955 of which were held by homesteaders. This left 3,255,045 acres yet available, a vast empire over which the cowmen ranged their herds, estimated by Oklahoma's territorial Governor C. B. Barnes at 75,171 cattle and 11,005 sheep.

Within four years, however, there was another rush for Beaver County homesteads, no doubt brought about by the extension of the Frisco Railroad across the county and the occupation of available free lands in adjacent states. By 1907, Beaver County's population had grown to 35,000 and all the best farmland was occupied. Drastic changes came with this settler tide, one of which was the springing up of ambitious new towns. "Guymon is the largest town in the county," wrote Tom Braidwood. "It is situated near the geographical center of the Panhandle [and later the dust bowl], and when the county is divided it will be the county seat of the middle county. It is striving for a land office with some show of success; churches of all denominations are represented; it has good schools. ... Beaver is the county seat with 250 people," he claimed for his home town. "It has three newspapers." Then he mentioned Kenton, the Panhandle's third largest town, and Tyrone, Goodwell, and Texhoma, as "new towns forging to the front."

Beaver citizens had enviously watched the rise of neighboring railroad towns. They knew that they must have a railroad if they maintained their urban leadership of the Panhandle. But how? In 1907 they joined with residents of the southeastern part of the county to organize the Beaver Valley and Northwestern Railroad Company to survey a road from Gage, through Beaver, to Liberal; but their plan failed.

This did not stop them. In the past they had driven out road trotters and cattle thieves, organized a territory, and built up their own institutions, and they did not intend to give up now. Therefore, they decided to build their own road. Business and professional men dug deep into their pockets for their savings; farmers contributed their share, furnishing teams and labor; and other town residents volunteered their services. By such a co-operative effort they built the roadbed through the deep sand beyond the Beaver River to Forgan. Then with justifiable pride they offered their partly completed project to the Missouri, Kansas and Texas Railroad Company (M. K. & T.), if it would complete it. But their offer was rejected. Frank Kell, promoter of the Wichita Falls and Northwestern, was building from northern Texas into the county via Woodward, reportedly under the sponsorship of the M. K. & T., and neither he nor his backers favored the Beaver City enterprise.

But Jacob Achenbaugh and Ira Blackstock, railroad men of Hardtner, Kansas, came to the rescue. Achenbaugh supplied much-needed funds and took over the road, and Blackstock superintended construction. After this, in 1930, the road was built from Forgan through Hooker to Keys, one hundred miles from Beaver, through a rich wheat belt.

Beaver citizens could now move ahead happily, knowing that their road was assured. They completed the project and began a regular train service; and the road, which no company would accept as a free gift, paid well from the beginning. It served as an important feeder for the M. K. & T. and the officials of that road offered to accept the long-standing Beaver proposal, but Achenbaugh refused them. He expressed a willingness to transfer the road if he were paid $2,200,000. The M. K. & T. officials had no other choice, since the road was a vital feeder to their own, and ruefully paid the price asked—$2,200,000 for a short line that at one time could have been theirs for the taking.

Hooker also profited by the completion of the Beaver, Meade, and Englewood, now a branch line of the M. K. & T., for it provided its farmers with another outlet for their wheat. The Rock Island Railroad had been their main dependence. Boise City, too, had railroad service when the Santa Fé, building southwest across the Panhandle, reached that place on October 2, 1925, and the population of the town leaped from 350 to 1,256 by 1930.

The building of railroads and the lure of free lands had brought tens of thousands of settlers into the territories of Oklahoma and the Five Civilized Tribes, as well as in to Beaver County. The Indians had asked for a state of their own to be called Sequoyah, but Congress had decided to join their Indian Territory and Oklahoma Territory to make the new state of Oklahoma. Beaver County sent Fred C. Tracy and T. C. James as its delegates to the constitutional convention held at Guthrie in 1906, which, among other acts, carved from the Panhandle the three present counties of Beaver, Texas, and Cimarron. Beaver City and Guymon became the county seats of the first two counties respectively; but in Cimarron several towns—Boise City, Cimarron, Doby, Garlington, and Hurley—were candidates for this honor. In the election of August 26, 1908, Boise City won. Goodwell residents supported Boise City's claims under a gentlemen's agreement that it in turn should have a proposed agricultural and mechanical college to be located in the Panhandle. In the next year Goodwell was given the new school, which started its first session in a downtown bank building while its first structure, Franklin Hall, was under construction.

Meanwhile, Panhandle farmers had renewed their efforts to grow wheat, probably induced to do so by the importation of drought-resisting wheat and improved farm machinery. In 1902–1903, Sam Kerns, near Gate City, for two years in succession reaped thirty bushels of wheat to the acre; Tom Buchanan, on Clear Creek, in southern Beaver County, twenty-two bushels to the acre; and Leonard Light, near present Barrouzett, harvested a crop of three thousand bushels. Farther west, in 1903, G. W. Riffe, of Tyrone, sowed the first wheat in that section of Texas County; and three years later, J. E. Patton built the first elevator there.

These initial successes caused other farmers to plant

wheat, although they continued to depend on such other crops as kaffir, maize, and broomcorn; however, for several years they met with indifferent success because of recurring drought. Still, those who had gained at wheat farming repeated their efforts, and at last they had a good crop year. There was small acreage in 1906, but the yield was fair. Then 1910 brought another good crop, pouring its golden wealth into Panhandle granaries. Four years later, upon the outbreak of the first World War, Panhandle wheat scored a sensational success; and with war prices, farmers forgot early privations.

Now began a mad gamble in land and wheat, not only in the Panhandle, but throughout the wheat belt of the Great Plains. W. I. Drummond in 1914 wrote of attending the International Dry Farming Congress at Wichita, Kansas, of which he was chairman. There the farmers were told of scientific methods to employ in semiarid fields, how to conserve the rainfall, to guard against erosion, and to rebuild worn-out land. A delegation of Kansas farmers listened attentively to all suggestions and inspected the experiment-station exhibits. Then their leader turned to Drummond and said: "We know all those things. We have learned them from experience. We know how to farm better than we do farm. We simply take chances, winning in good seasons, and losing when it fails to rain, or if the wind blows out our crops."

What this Kansan meant to say was that Great Plains farmers were willing to sow the wind and take their chances against reaping the whirlwind. If they lost, they would not be much poorer; but if they won, riches would be theirs. Moved by this thought, they gambled recklessly; and land values boomed and wheat prices soared to the dizzy height of $2.75 per bushel. The momentum of the boom carried into the period of reconstruction, for hungry Europeans must be fed.

Land values continued high, as seen in the Goodwell *Independent* of July 20, 1920. "Our old friend, Bird McDaniel," the editor chided, "is moving to Stratford, Texas, this week having bought some land there. He sold his farm here at Goodwell a few months ago for $75.00 per acre and his wheat off the same place paid him the sum of $79.30 per acre!" He added that Harry Daniels of Sublette had grown enough wheat on sixty-five acres to pay for his 160-acre claim; and W. R. Treece, near Texhoma, had realized enough from the sale of his crop to pay out his place with 931 bushels of wheat left to buy another quarter-section of land.

Avis D. Carlson condemned "suit-case farmers"—shopkeepers, bankers, and lawyers "in one thousand little towns" who swarmed out to buy Western land. "Often they did not put a tenant on it but bought power machinery and hired a mechanic to run it. In Kansas and Colorado the jump in wheat acreage was astounding. In 1926, Hamilton County, Kansas, had 10,000 acres in wheat; five years later, 104,835 acres in wheat. In a neighboring county of Greeley, the wheat acreage in 1931 was almost as much as the total land in farms twenty years earlier."

Many Panhandle landholders joined this land-grabbing movement; vast waving fields of golden wheat promised great wealth. In 1917, E. O. Love of Tyrone, sold in that vicinity alone, 190 combines. The rush for wheat acreage was accentuated still more when in 1924 and 1926 the wheat yield ranged from twenty-five to seventy bushels to the acre!

This remarkable success caused machine farming to supplant horsepower farming and a new era to roll in on combines, reapers, and tractors. Early homesteaders could not foresee these extraordinary times, when it was quite common for a farmer to operate one thousand or more acres and harvest many thousands of bushels of wheat. On December 13, 1928, the *Panhandle Herald* (Guymon) gave this list of its bonanza farmers and their wheat yields: "H. S. Hawkins and sons, 46,000 bushels from 1,900 acres; J. H. Gruver, 110,000 bushels of wheat and 17,000 bushels of barley from 4,000 acres; M. E. Bergner, 42,000 bushels of wheat; and F. N. Hemphill, 36,000 bushels from 1,200 acres."

Such large-scale successes called for more land and more machines. On mechanized farming, the *Herald's* editor mentioned C. W. E. Bergner's farm near Texhoma, where "he had three combines hauled by tractors in operation, and two tractor-drawn one-way discs following the combines, and being operated day and night to prepare the land for the next year's crop." This technique was followed also by other Panhandle wheat farmers.

Occasional droughts went unheeded. The wheat farmers' large investments had been predicated on lucrative returns. The *New York Times* (magazine section) of March 31, 1935, criticized this choice, stating that land plowed recklessly during the World War and since, denuded of vegetation which knits the earth against the onslaughts of the winds, powdered by drought for years, would one day take wing. For a time, however, their land did not fail them. Texas County alone produced upward of 12,000,000 bushels of wheat in 1928. Then what the wheat farmer should have expected, happened: the market was glutted. In 1931 some discouraged Panhandle farmers sold wheat for twenty-two cents per bushel. Many farmers could not keep up their gamble and fell by the wayside. They had the added cost of fuel and labor beyond high interest rates on borrowed capital and excessively priced farm machinery. The debacle of 1931 wrought havoc throughout the wheat belt; but there was only the hard way to recoup, the embattled farmers thought—raise more wheat and buy more land.

And here again Nature opposed them. W. I. Drummond tells of an experience in farming while he was a lad. One day while he was planting corn on a Beaver farm, a cowman quietly watched him. "We have good corn land here," young Drummond remarked. "Yes son," the rancher answered, "but you haven't got a corn sky" —a truth that the young farmer always remembered. Drought was the sword of Damocles over the Panhandle farmer's head.

Reaping the Whirlwind

Millions of acres of South-
ern Plains farmland had been plowed up for the first time
by wheat farmers during the nineteen twenties and the
nineteen thirties that were best suited for ranching. Much
of this was thin land, dry land, and mostly out of bounds
of the proved dry-farming territory. Worse still, the plow-
man did little to conserve and rebuild the soil and to
study his growing problem of erosion.

Nor could Panhandle residents say that they had no
warning of impending disaster. As early as 1893 an awe-
some dust storm broke over the recently settled and partly
plowed Cherokee Outlet and Beaver County; and an
even more sinister sky monster winged in during the
spring of 1895. The Alva *Review* of April 11 carried a
graphic account of this appalling phenomenon, stating
that the rain which followed in its wake "became a veritable shower of mud, turning the north side of the town's
brick buildings into a dirty, drab color." "The color of
the dust," stated the editor, "indicated that it was for-
eign and came with the storm from the north."

Recurring and similar dust storms supported the de-
structiveness of water erosion, to whip loose plowed soil,
including the rich humus, from the ground and dump

it into Southern Plains streams, causing such beautiful rivers as the Beaver and the Cimarron to become sluggish, muddy rivulets, flowing over wide, sandy beds; and their tributaries to be little more than dry arroyos except during rain storms. Harry Parker stated that earlier "the creeks were narrow, rippling streams with elm, cottonwood, willow, hackberry and chinaberry trees growing along their banks. There were deep pools in these creeks which were full of fine fish." Still Mother Nature's warning was disregarded, and the farmer's plow bit hungrily into virgin sod.

Guymon had a preview of the "Dirty Thirties" at 4:30 o'clock on a Saturday afternoon in March, 1923. In the north and west was a great bank of what seemed to be reddish-brown and blue-black clouds, which boiled, rolled, and tumbled silently, like seething smoke caused by oil fires and explosions. Rapidly this pall of clouds covered a large scope of the horizon, making many watchers frantic with fear as they ran for shelter. Within a short space of time all cellars in town were crowded. But other men watched awe-stricken until a blanket of inky darkness engulfed them. An automobile light was not visible a few feet away. Blinding, choking dust settled on the watchers and sent them gasping to their homes. "The wind must have carried this great volume of dust high in the air," the editor of the *Herald* theorized, "for gradually it settled down until a gale was sweeping through the streets of the town. The intense darkness lasted for more than an hour and then [the sun] gradually began to appear, first in a hazy brown, until finally, about six o'clock, the sun was peeping through the dust in rays of a fiery red hue."

Progress of a dust storm at Guymon, 1937
(continued on next page

Progress of a dust storm at Guymon, 1937

For the next ten years the Panhandle farmers met with varying fortune. There were years of plenty and years of drought and poverty. They learned to carry surpluses of fat years over to lean years; but no one was prepared to meet the prolonged drought of the "Dirty Thirties," not even the most experienced plainsmen.

During 1933 there were the usual spring dust storms and then quieter summer days, although dry and hot, with the thermometer registering as high as 110 degrees. But there was no rain. Later, the fall and winter winds pushed dark clouds of dust over the Southern Plains, in large part from out-of-bounds, thin, and submarginal lands, with still no rain or snow. Deeply plowed wheat fields, naked and plantless, greeted the gusty spring of the next year, with loose topsoil ready to take wing in flight.

As early as March, black blizzards shrieked across the barren land, piling up sand dunes in unexpected places and increasing in intensity through April. Then came the black day of April 12, 1934, in which, according to Department of Agriculture estimates, the wind lifted 300,000,000 tons of soil off the Great Plains, carried a part of it eastward at a height of two to three miles, and spilled it into the Atlantic. Secretary Henry A. Wallace was appalled. "On May 12, 1934," he later said, "for the first time since white men came to America, we had a great dust storm that originated in the plains country near the foot of the Rocky Mountains and swept across the continent and far out to sea. It deposited rich Western soil on the window ledges of New York skyscrapers and on the Capitol in Washington."

The following year was equally dismal. One dust storm followed another during the early spring months.

Harlan Miller's graphic narrative, in the *New York Times* of March 31, of a "gray duster" told how dust from the Great Plains spattered "volcanic granules across state papers at the White House, dusted Manhattan sky-scrapers and Long Island estates with fugitive real estate from Texas and New Mexico."

The following April was worse. "If an attorney should ever ask a resident of Beaver County, Oklahoma, 'Where were you on April 14, 1935?'" wrote Mrs. A. C. Guffy, "the answer will not be 'I don't remember,' circumstances of that date are fixed by the dust storm that arrived at Beaver City about 4 o'clock in the afternoon."

Without warning, a dark cloud rose on the northern horizon, extending by a wide arch from east to west; and it approached rapidly and silently, boiling and rolling like a giant monster in mortal pain. Its top part was a brownish-gray, but near the earth it was as black as midnight. The silence of death settled on the earth as this seething, monstrous catastrophe blotted out the blue sky with its blackness of doom. Like hope's negation and terrible chaos, the cloud rolled over the prairies.

"Hundreds of geese and ducks and smaller birds too numerous to count," wrote A. A. Justice of Dodge City, "were racing for their lives. . . . The almost entire absence of all birds following the storm was one proof of its severity."

Darkness such as Beaver City residents had never known in daytime came on the van of a sighing breeze. For a time people watched in sheer terror this monstrous thing; then they fled to their storm cellars and homes to escape what seemed impending doom. Yet they knew that there was no escape. For the first time, some felt an unreasoning, hopeless despair, knowing that they were in stygian darkness, so dark that electric-light globes gleamed faintly, like candles. H. J. Crabtree made his way to a window to raise the shade for light, and his hand touched glass instead of the window shade. Young Tom Peckham blindly groped his way homeward. He stumbled on a fence and followed it blindly, touched a building, felt his way to a window and rapped on it, calling the name of his neighbor. But he had reached home, and a member of his family rescued him.

Total darkness lasted for about two hours. Then it gradually passed, first giving place to a bloodlike dawn, with the sun like a ball of molten fire riding low in the western sky. It was a strange world that the incredulous Beaver residents looked upon. Dust had cast its gray pall over everything—drooping trees, the red clay streets, dainty white tables and mantel pieces, bed covers, floors, and kitchens. Dust had sifted through cracks and crannies, window sills, and door frames to choke and stifle those within the houses.

This was only the first of the black blizzards that swept the High Plains during the long, weary months to follow. Sand like huge snowdrifts blocked roads, submerged tractors, plows, and wagons standing in the fields, and covered fences and low sheds. Cows had to eat drought-parched grass and weeds piercing through a mantle of sand, showing here and there; in places plowed fields were denuded of rich humus, and in other places showed with remarkable distinctness the fingering patterns of wind ripples.

The Panhandle dug out of this dust spread, only to repeat, again and again, its digging. People learned to calk their windows and doors to keep out the dust. The

Boise City *News* of April 25, 1935, stated that masks were quite the vogue, that a Dexter, Missouri, farm lad had worn a homemade mask and equipped his horse with a sand-proof *morral* or nosebag. Some Panhandle towns offered masks for sale in shades to suit the purchasers.

Mrs. Caroline A. Henderson, writing from Eva, in Texas County, in the heart of the dust bowl, on April 6, 1937, poured out in plaintive sentences a striking story. "High winds and consequent dust storms began early this year," she wrote, "and still continue at frequent intervals. While perhaps no more violent than the storms of previous years, their effects, being cumulative, seem more disastrous and overwhelming. On some days the limit of vision has been a row of little elms about thirty feet from the front windows. No eye could penetrate any farther the swirling blinding clouds of dust which made Monday as dark as late twilight of a clear evening. The worst storm thus far in 1937 occurred immediately after a slight snowfall which again aroused delusive hopes. That snow melted on Tuesday; Wednesday morning, with a rising wind, the dust soon began to move again, and until late Friday night there was little respite.

"Almost as distressing are the more frequent days when the northward-creeping sun shines faintly above the dizzying drift of silt, ground to a fine whitish powder, which gives a ghastly appearance of unreality to the most familiar landscapes. On such days we suffer from a painful sense of helplessness and utter frustration. We need no Calendar to tell us that planting time is here again. The cranes went north some time ago." But the common misery in which all life shared seemed to make her more sensitive to suffering life. "Another blinded rabbit," she

184

wrote, "picked up in the yard has just died in spite of all my care. When these wild creatures, ordinarily so well able to take care of themselves, come seeking protection, this necessity indicates a cruel crisis for man and beast."

Her worst trial, however, was yet ahead. Sixty-one dust storms had scourged the Panhandle in 1935, forty-five in 1936, and sixty in 1937. Seventy-one others were to come in the next year, stifling and blinding, and so far reaching as to imperil the whole nation. Yet Nature seemed to put its final supreme effort in the greatest of them all—the black blizzard of March 11, 1939. Dr. W. B. Gernert, agronomist of the Oklahoma Agricultural and Mechanical College, pronounced it the worst. It brought upon the state a staggering blanket of dust, weighing 198,117,270,072 pounds. "If dust landed all over the state equally as dense as at Stillwater," reasoned a writer for the *Daily Oklahoman* (Oklahoma City), "Doctor Gernert figures 4,779,320 acres of land, one foot deep, left the 'dust bowl' and moved to Oklahoma."

By 1940 rain drummed out the good news of better days for the dust bowl. Throughout the long years of drought and dust, the Panhandle had again become a veritable No Man's Land. Now desperately sick, physically, mentally, and economically, it climbed out of its dust heap, although painfully. The region was a desert as compared with its golden wheat years; and its people were in flight.

Following the first great dust storm of April, 1935, several families from Beaver County arrived at Boise City en route to Oregon. Members of one family had become "sanded" and were forced to leave; the others had become discouraged and had left to seek more promising locations. Lawrence Svobida stated that the California Department of Agriculture had counted 221,000 persons entering that state in motor vehicles belonging to families looking for work and that 94 per cent of these had come from the drought-stricken states. Similarly, in the same year, 60 per cent of drought-stricken people entered Oregon, and 57 per cent, Washington. And as the drought continued, the exodus increased.

Two years later Mrs. Henderson drove from Eva to Guymon, a distance of thirty miles. She said that she could count only sixteen occupied homes, including those within half a mile on either side of the federal highway. Thomas Alfred Tripp told much the same story upon a revisit to a part of the dust bowl. "Instead of a family on nearly every 160-acre tract," he said, "as was the case fifteen years ago, there is hardly one occupied farmstead to a section. . . . The displaced farmers have left the state or have gone to town, many of them to get on relief."

John Steinbeck hardly overplayed the "Okies" in his *Grapes of Wrath,* as abundant contemporary evidence shows. But those who trekked from western Texas, western Kansas, western Nebraska—indeed, from the whole dust bowl—were equally forlorn and poverty ridden. Many, in fact, were ill. In its *Report* of 1935, the Kansas State Board of Health stated that the dust storms were not only terrifying but destructive to property, death to small creatures, and detrimental to human health, concluding that the dust storms' ill effects came from silica breathed by its victims. "Since the dust storms of last spring," its report ran, "Kansas has had the worst measles epidemic in its history. Acute lung-infections have increased considerably; pneumonia rates have gone up 100

per cent. Eye and throat diseases, attributable to after-
effects of the dust storms, have given public health officials
concern." No doubt the health problem continued to be
acute throughout the next four years.

The finest Christmas present ever received by the
dust-bowl people was a fourteen-inch snow in 1939. This
was followed by soaking rains in April, and the Panhandle
wheat crop, estimated at 25,470,000 bushels before the
rains, finally produced 46,763,000 bushels.

But more than rain and snow were necessary to re-
store this new No Man's Land to its former economy.
Hundreds of sand dunes must be leveled, soil-rebuilding
crops planted, and erosion stopped. It was no easy task,
for the region involved comprised 90,000 square miles,
according to the *Daily Oklahoman* of September 11,
1938; but by this date "all but 4,000 square miles of the
desolate, windswept area of Kansas, Colorado, Oklahoma,
Texas, and New Mexico had been reclaimed for produc-
tion." This was premature optimism, for, as has been said,
the worst dust storm of all struck during the spring of the
next year.

The federal government had spent $250,000,000 to
promote recovery. Nevertheless, wide areas of the dust
bowl were still strewn with sand dunes, ranging from
fifty to more than eight hundred yards in length, twenty
to thirty yards in width, and some as high as twenty-six
feet. In August, 1934, the federal government set up a
control project near Dalhart, Texas, and within three
years twenty-six similar projects were started in the same
area. The primary object was to level the dunes and re-
claim the land by cover crops such as broomcorn, Sudan
grass, kaffir, and hegari. At the end of 1937 soil conserva-

tionists announced that out of 28,765 acres in the Dalhart region, 25,025 had been stabilized.

States joined with the federal government in reclaiming their waste lands. Various methods were used. Strip farming (e. g., planting alternate strips of kaffir and wheat), building lakes and ponds, retiring tilled land to grass, resettlement of those living on submarginal lands, planting of trees, and the introduction of new varieties of cover crops—all were tried.

Mrs. Henderson wrote hopefully of federal aid in the Eva community. She said that a farmer who was willing to co-operate with the government might select 15 per cent of his cropland to follow in cultivation one of several soil-conservation methods, and agree to leave on the ground for protective purposes whatever crop was produced upon that acreage. For his labor, seed, and sacrifice of any harvested crop, he was offered $6.40 per acre for first-class land.

With the other 85 per cent of his acreage, he could do as he liked, though in case of negligence which menaced the farms of others, any expected benefits were forfeited. Should one desire to go beyond the minimum conservation plan and increase his Class I payment, he might choose from thirty-three methods to be applied to his 85 per cent acreage, and thus become eligible for payments from twenty cents to seventy-five cents per acre. "The combination of the two types of payment on a basis of 100 acres of cultivation," she estimated, "might amount to a maximum of $174.75," although she felt that this should not be encouraged as a purely monetary objective.

Frankly, no one can speak with authority on the future of the Dust Bowl. The two great control factors are the weather and the proper use of marginal lands. If adequate rain falls, good crops are reasonably certain and dangers of dust storms slight. It should be remembered that the prolonged drought of the "Dirty Thirties" was a meteorological phenomenon that had never before afflicted the Great Plains during the white man's occupation. Undoubtedly J. Gilbert Hill is at least in part right when he says that "neither man nor the Government 'controlled' the blowing fields. Nature did," for the great drought was followed by wet years and the high prices of the recent war. He believes that "when it turns dry again the dust will blow again." Others say not. Time alone will prove who is right.

The period of the drought brought a fourth sifting of the Panhandle population, as seen on the accompanying census chart. Particularly in Beaver and Texas counties, the major wheat-growing belt, the drop in the number of farms from 1935 to 1940 is large.

If the hot-wind scourge of 1893 was a "trial by fire," the "Dirty Thirties" represented a trial by dust and a more terrific ordeal. It is more surprising and significant that thousands of people stayed and endured the dust storms than that thousands of "Okies" fled. A Boise City resident stated that the Panhandle was "no place for sissies," implying, as still another believed, that "it takes a generation to live out here."

No sturdier, resourceful people live on the American continent today than those of old No Man's Land. Like the hardy wind-blown and fiber-toughened plant of the desert, they have survived every test to build a progressive culture. If one should ask why old No Man's Land was not entirely depopulated during the last prolonged drought, Miss Maude O. Thomas of Beaver City, speaking in 1936, answered: "Do they intend to leave the Promised Land where sleep their brave pioneer fathers and mothers? No, a thousand times, No! . . . This, too, will pass, and again we shall see our verdant hills and vales in all their beauty, and our wide expanse of golden grain waving in the mellow glow of twilight."

You can't beat a faith like that. The Panhandle will survive many another scourge when it is controlled by this spirit.

Census Data Showing Agricultural Changes During Settlement and Dust Storm Period, in the Panhandle of Oklahoma

ACREAGE

CIMARRON COUNTY

Year	No. Farms	Crop Land	Wheat	Sorghum Grain	Sorghum Forage
1910	1,307	117,828*	2,496	------	------
1920	767	97,179*	15,054	35,282	16,131
1925	761	148,319	50,377	32,965	13,826
1930	887	315,513	175,903	27,438	12,901
1935	975	425,595	90,064	2,459	5,955
1940	605	351,767	60,467	41,188	17,742

TEXAS COUNTY

Year	No. Farms	Crop Land	Wheat	Sorghum Grain	Sorghum Forage
1910	3,026	456,356*	48,732	------	------
1920	2,266	528,799*	151,380	129,807	49,148
1925	2,288	501,975	222,722	115,381	37,826
1930	2,020	675,717	475,478	58,038	22,490
1935	2,135	752,041	352,903	6,188	21,588
1940	1,408	685,708	204,723	33,184	24,361

BEAVER COUNTY

Year	No. Farms	Crop Land	Wheat	Sorghum Grain	Sorghum Forage
1910	3,568	487,893*	64,893	------	------
1920	2,518	508,103*	154,507	140,075	49,824
1925	2,375	441,988	196,862	78,969	36,065
1930	2,047	520,855	328,572	47,431	30,538
1935	2,080	547,025	125,410	3,062	37,022
1940	1,659	514,455	196,066	29,137	30,979

* Classed as improved land. Data furnished by H. H. Finnell, research specialist, Soil Conservation Service, United States Department of Agriculture, Amarillo, Texas.

BIBLIOGRAPHY

1. MANUSCRIPTS

The National Archives, Washington, D. C., are the most important depository of No Man's Land manuscripts and printed documents. These materials are varied, consisting of fifty or more letters, reports, statistics, petitions, and maps. Two archives, the Interior Department and the Justice Department, are most abundant. In the Interior Department Archives, such categories as "Patents and Miscellaneous," "General Land Office, Townsite Cases," "Townsite Census," "Miscellaneous Letters Received, 1889–1894," and "Archives No. 22865" are self-explanatory. The Justice Department Archives carry the border people's complaints, memorials, and the correspondence of Kansas and Texas district attorneys and marshals with the attorney general.

In addition to these two important depositories, there are five others housing miscellaneous papers. Letters, memorials, and statistical data are found in the Legislative Records; records of the establishment of No Man's Land post offices and star routes, and the appointment of postmasters, in the Post Office Department Archives; correspondence relating to illicit distilleries and counterfeiters, in the Treasury Department Archives; miscellaneous papers, in the War Records Office; and interesting maps depicting No Man's Land from decade to decade, in the Division of Maps and Charts.

In the Fred S. Barde Collection, Oklahoma Historical

Library, Oklahoma City, are the sheets of the "First Territorial Census of Oklahoma, Population, 1890" (incomplete). Here also are found the "Record Book of Beaver, Neutral Strip, Indian Territory (No. 1), Nov. 29, 1886," and such other papers as a letter, David D. Collins to Fred S. Barde, May 8, 1909; I. S. Drummond's two articles, "A True Terra Incognito" and "No Man's Land;" and an unsigned manuscript, dated "Kenton, Ok., Sept. 12, 1910," relating to hunting in No Man's Land during the early eighteen seventies.

Beaver City citizens made available for the author's use abstract records, other manuscripts, papers, clippings, early-day photographs, and collected reminiscences. Most important is the "Journal of Proceedings, Hall Territorial Council, Beaver, Cimarron Territory, 1887," at present kept in a vault of a local bank. The Lawson Title Company has a collection of various kinds of materials bearing on No Man's Land. Among these are numerous newspaper clippings, more than 100 photographs, the personal narratives of J. H. Abbott, Thomas Judy, A. M. McCoy, Arthur M. Howe, Fred C. Tracy, and others. Mr. Tracy also supplied the author with other papers and early photographs, and Mr. W. T. Quinn, with the "Life Story of James Riley Quinn."

Luke Cahill's eyewitness narrative (72 pages, Colorado Historical Museum, Denver) is valuable for its details relating to western No Man's Land, the brigand Coe, Robber's Roost, and for the hunting of buffalo during the late eighteen sixties. Equally important is the diary of the late Boss Neff of Hooker on ranching and life in central No Man's Land; and the memoirs of Mr. and Mrs. Harry Parker of Follett, Texas, regarding pioneer life near old Sod Town.

In the Indian-Pioneer Papers of the Phillips Collection of the University of Oklahoma the author found the accounts of M. A. Willoughby, v. 99, 75–76; Marion Albert Yoakum, v. 101, 17–22; Arthur Black, v. 8, 210–12; James Frederick

Beecham, v. 6, 202–206; James Hamford Flint, v. 30, 320–21; Etta Dale, v. 23, 34; C. W. Chadwick, v. 17, 470–71; Jim England, v. 28, 78–83; Mary S. England, v. 28, 91; Jack N. Innis, v. 46, 413–15; A. E. Enfield, v. 28, 71–72; Ed Hughes, v. 45, 208–209; Bill Ewing, v. 28, p. 149; Bill Duncan, v. 26, 171; T. W. Howell, v. 44, 361–66; J. D. Sapp and Bill Ewing, v. 80, 207–208; and William Hogan, v. 43, 157–58.

2. PRINTED DOCUMENTS

Agricultural Statistics (1930–40), United States Department of Agriculture, federal census returns (1880–1940), *Annual Reports,* Oklahoma territorial governors (1891–1906) —all show the ebb and flow of the No Man's Land population, the occupied and unoccupied lands, and property values. Miscellaneous items are found in other documents. A sketch of the "Public Land Strip" is carried in the *Annual Report of the General Land Office for the Year 1889* (Washington, 1889), 62–63; an excellent brief of the Haystack affair, in *The Supreme Court of the United States, October Term, 1890, C. E. Cook et al;* the New Mexico–Oklahoma Panhandle Boundary problem, in *Appendex, Congressional Globe,* 35 Congress, 1 session, 565–66; and Chase's petition to Congress in *Congressional Record,* 50 Congress, 1 session, 38–40. In addition, the Kansas Adjutant General's *Annual Reports* occasionally refer to conditions in No Man's Land. For example, the reports of 1879, pp. 34–35, of 1882, and of 1885, p. 45, deal at length with the cowmen's "Indian scare"; and that of 1888, pp. 66–79, 404, with the "Stevens County-seat Trouble" (the Haystack affair).

3. NEWSPAPERS

The Cheyenne Transporter, (Darlington, Indian Territory) August 25, 1880–August 12, 1886; the *Hardesty Herald* (Territory of Oklahoma), May 31–August 16, 1890, and January 4, 1895–July 31, 1896; the *Beaver Advocate* (Beaver County, Oklahoma Territory), January 26, 1893–December 28, 1893; the *Beaver County Democrat* (Beaver City, Oklahoma Territory), June 9, 1893–June 28, 1894, and July 5, 1894–July 26, 1894; the Woodward *Jeffersonian* (Oklahoma Territory), September 30, 1893, then from July 21, 1894–July 19, 1895; Alva *Review* (Oklahoma Territory), July 7, 1894–October 11, 1894, and March 28 to Dec. 29, 1895; the Colorado (Texas) *Clipper,* December 25, 1884–October 31, 1895; Garden City (Kansas) *Herald,* 1886–90; Garden City (Kansas) *Lookout,* August, 1891–October 15, 1892; Dodge City (Kansas) *Champion,* July–September, 1887; Dodge City (Kansas) *Democrat,* December 29, 1883–May 19, 1889; and *Ford County Republican* (Dodge City) 1887–1889; Canadian (Texas) *Crescent,* January, 1888–June 1889; Topeka (Kansas) *Commonwealth,* January 2–15, 1886.

Newspapers from which single references or quotations are taken are cited only in the narrative.

4. PERIODICALS

Abel, Anna Heloise. "Indian Reservations in Kansas and the Extinguishment of their Title," *Kansas Historical Collections,* vol. VIII (1903–1904), 79.

"A Tragedy and Trial of No Man's Land," *Green Bag,* vol. IX (1897), 494.

Beck, T. E. "Cimarron Territory," *Chronicles of Oklahoma,* vol. VII (June, 1929), 169.

Brown, Elmer E. "No Man's Land," *Chronicles of Oklahoma,* vol. IV (June, 1926), 89–99.

Byers, Oliver Philip. "Early History of the El Paso Line of the Chicago, Rock Island and Pacific Railway," *Kansas Historical Collections,* vol. XV (1919–22), 576.

Carlson, Avis D. "Dust Blowing," *The Nation,* vol. 171 (June–November, 1935), 149–58.

Drummond. "Short Grass Country—where dry years and high winds speed the errant soil, and only nature can bring relief to stout-hearted dust bowl farmers," *Review of Reviews,* vols. 93–94 (June, 1936), 37–40.

"Dust Storms Aftermath," *The Literary Digest,* vol. 120 (November 2, 1936), 15.

Frederick, J. V. "The Vigilantes in Early Beaver," *Chronicles of Oklahoma,* vol. XVI (June, 1938), 190–96.

Gould, Charles M. "Dedication of Monument on Black Mesa," *Oklahoma Chronicles,* vol. VII (March, 1929), 34–54.

Henderson, Caroline A. "Spring in the Dust Bowl," the *Atlantic Monthly,* vol. 159 (January–June, 1937), 715–17.

Hill, J. Gilbert. "Plains Will Blow Again," *Science Digest,* vol. XVII (January–June, 1945), 89–92.

Holden, W. C. "Coronado's Route Across the Staken Plains," *West Texas Historical Association Yearbook,* vol. XX (October, 1944), 3–21.

Kunigunde, Duncan. "Reclaiming the Dust Bowl," *The Nation,* vol. 149 (June–December, 1939), 269–71.

Judy, H. S. "No Man's Land," *The Cattleman,* July, 1939.

Kinchen, Oscar A. "Pioneers in No Man's Land" *West Texas Historical Association Yearbook,* vol. XVIII (October, 1942), 24–32.

Malin, James C. "Dust Storms, 1850–1900," *Kansas Historical Quarterly,* vol. XIV (May, August, November, 1946), 1–16, 17–48, 49–71 (reprint).

Nough, E. "The Last Buffalo Hunt," *The Kansas Magazine,* vol. VI (January, 1887), 212–13.

Overstreet, Rev. R. M. "The Story of No Man's Land," *Sturms's Magazine,* vol. V (January, 1908), 53–60; and (February, 1908), 17–23.

———"Influence of the Church in No Man's Land," *ibid.,* vol. VII (December, 1908), 65–70.

Painter, J. S. (ed. Garden City *Herald*). "Southwest Kansas," *Kansas Historical Transactions,* vol. IV (1886–1888), 281–86.

Spears, J. R. "Story of No Man's Land," *Chautaquah,* vol. X (October–March, 1889–90), 176.

Thompson, Albert W. "Kit Carson's Camp Nichols in No Man's Land," *Colorado Magazine,* vol. X (January, 1933), 179–86.

Tripp, Thomas Alfred. "Dust Bowl Tragedy," *Christian Century,* vol. 57 (January–June, 1940), 108–10.

Wardell, M. L., "The History of No Man's Land, or Old Beaver County," *Chronicles of Oklahoma,* vol. I (January, 1921), 60–89.

5. MISCELLANEOUS

Domenech, Abbe Em. *Seven Years Residence in the Great Deserts of North America.* London, 1860. 2 vols.

Gregg, Josiah. *Commerce of the Prairies.* New York, 1844; reprinted Cleveland, 1905. 2 vols.

Kennedy, William. *Texas: The Rise, Progress, and Prospects of the Republic of Texas.* London, 1841; reprinted, Fort Worth, Texas, 1925.

Lewis, Charles Brooks. "The Development of Cimarron County." Unpublished Master of Arts Thesis, University of Oklahoma. Norman, 1939.

Matthews, W. B. *The Settler's Map and Guide Book.* Washington, 1889.

McWilliams, Cary. *Ill Fares the Land, Migrants and Migratory Labor in the United States.* Boston, 1942.

Rainey, George. *No Man's Land.* Enid, 1937.

Risinger, Hurshal H. "Social and Economic Study of Texas County." Unpublished Master of Arts Thesis, University of Oklahoma. Norman, 1937.

Sears, Paul B. *Deserts on the March.* Norman, 1937.

Svobida, Lawrence. *An Empire of Dust.* Caldwell, Idaho, 1940.

Thoburn, Joseph B., and Wright, Muriel H. *Oklahoma. A History of the State and Its People.* New York, 1929. 4 vols. Vol. III, 522–26.

Wislizenus, Dr. A. "Memoir of a Tour in Northern Mexico," *Senate Miscellaneous Document,* No. 26, 30 Cong., 1 sess. (Serial 511).

INDEX

Abreu, Franco P.: encounters *comancheros,* 18
Achenbaugh, Jacob: Beaver railroad official, 173
Adobe Walls: Indians attack, 27
Allen, J. A.: estimates buffalo slaughter, 21
Allen, Rev. R. A.: Methodist minister, 66, 95
Alva *Review:* describes 1895 dust storm, 179

Battey, Thomas C.: describes buffalo stampede, 22
Beales, Dr. J. C.: claims part of No Man's Land, 10; Rio Grande colony, 11
Beaver City, Oklahoma: townsite company, 61–63; border town of, 62–66; leading citizens of, 65–66; establishment of, 63; cowboy pranks at, 84–86; first shooting at, 86; public dance at, 87–90; growth of, 94–95; Presbyterian church of, 95; officials, 113; mass meeting, 140; territorial government, 140 ff; Rothwell, a rival of, 146; improvement, 153; schools, 165–67; normal institute, 166; Fourth of July celebration (1893), 167–69; railroad survey through, 172; railroad promotion in, 172–73; M. K. & T. Railroad buys Beaver Railroad, 173; county seat of Beaver County, 174
Beaver County: area of, 171; Braidwood reports on, 171–72; creation of, 174
Beaver River: Santa Fé road crosses, 18; important to No Man's Land, 54–55
Beaver Valley and Northwestern Railroad Company: 172
Becknell, William: on Santa Fé Trail, 9